12 AMAZING FRANCHISE

OPPORTUNITIES

— for 2015 —

Praise for

12 Amazing Franchise Opportunities
— for 2015 —

"John Hayes's *12 Amazing Franchise Opportunities* provides crucial and critical information for those who aspire to fame and fortune in the wonderful world of franchising. He knows and expresses clearly and coherently most—if not all—of the many nuances there are in franchising. This is **a must read for those who are already franchisors and franchisees, but especially for those who aspire to become successful as either.**"

William B. Cherkasky, former President
International Franchise Association
Former Executive Director
U. S. Senate Committee on Small Business

"Dr. Hayes has an amazing ability to uncomplicate the franchise buying process. He's able to provide invaluable insight in the entire selection and purchase process. **Dr. Hayes provides a road map, which simplifies what would otherwise be a difficult and confusing process.**"

Tom Portesy, President
MFV Expositions

"It was through my involvement with International Franchise Association that I came to know and respect John Hayes, author of this book. John has been a featured lecturer at many IFA events, both from the perspective of the franchisor and the franchisee. He is **an acknowledged industry expert**. I have listened to his advice and if you are thinking about investing in a franchise, you should, too."

Gary Goranson
Founder and former CEO of Tidy Car
Founder and owner of WorkEnders, Inc.
Coach and creator of www.HouseCleaningBiz101.com

Dr. John Hayes is the world's leading authority on franchising. I know him as a franchisor, and when thinking about franchising our company he was my first call. **You shouldn't make a franchise decision without reading everything Dr. Hayes has written on franchising.**

J. Barry Watts, CEO
WealthCare Investment Advisors

"John's book is a must read for all prospective franchisees around the world. Most importantly, one must ask whether he/she knows what franchising entails, and whether he/she has the personality, resources and commitment to work with the franchisor to achieve the desired success."

Albert Kong (CFE, CMC, Senior PMC)
Chairman/CEO
Asiawide Franchise Consultants Pte Ltd

"This is a fascinating book about a wide variety of franchising opportunities. If you want a road map to a new life in business, **this is the book you must read!"**

Mary Ellen Sheets, Founder
Two Men & A Truck

"John Hayes is **without question one of the world's foremost authorities** on the subject of franchising and one of the most prolific and pertinent authors in this field. Congratulations on yet another **informative and valuable resource book!"**

Chris M. Levano, President
Quality Restaurant Consulting, Ltd.

"This one book should be read by every single franchise company and every single entrepreneur thinking of buying a franchise.... **Everything this man writes or speaks I implement into my practice."**

Mike Cheves, CEO
Hurricane Group, Inc.

"Coming from a thirty-year franchise veteran, *12 Amazing Franchise Opportunities for 2015*, is **one of the most profound and insightful publications I have ever read.**"

"John Hayes's *12 Amazing Franchise Opportunities for 2015* serves as not only a primer for those interested in launching their own business, but also as an idea book that underscores the variety of opportunities that exist for wannabe business owners. A mobile dentistry repair unit? It's working and making money for franchisees. Hayes explains the concept of that and 11 other franchises that are waiting to come to your town. **Spending a weekend with this book might just change your life.**"

"Excellent, and to the point book! John is the consummate franchise expert and teacher. If you're serious about becoming a franchise business owner, then use this book as **your guidebook to the best franchising opportunities available today.**"

"**FIVE STARS! and a must read for anyone thinking about buying a franchise.** John Hayes makes clear what you must know about successful franchising. He points out 12 terrific franchise opportunities: how each was developed and why it is so good is explained. This proven expert makes it easy to see if franchising is right for you, and what type of franchising will be best. Included are questions you should always ask, plus step-by-step guidance for making a good buying decision. Another great book on franchising by this author."

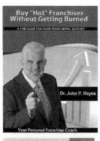

A few other books by
John P. Hayes, Ph.D.

Buy "Hot" Franchises Without Getting Burned

101 Questions to Ask Before You Invest in a Franchise

Start Small Finish Big
(with the co-founder of Subway restaurants)

Mooney: Life of the World's Master Carver

Network Marketing for Dummies
(with Zig Ziglar)

James A. Michener: A Biography

Philadelphia in Color

You Can't Teach a Kid to Ride a Bike at a Seminar
(with David Sandler)

Taming Your Turmoil
(with Dr. Peter Brill)

How to Win Productivity in Manufacturing
(with William E. Sandman)

12 AMAZING FRANCHISE OPPORTUNITIES

OPPORTUNITIES

— for 2015 —

Compiled by

Dr. John P. Hayes

12 Amazing Franchise Opportunities for 2015

ISBN: 978-0-9897670-4-0

First edition published 2014

BizCom Press
A division of BizCom Associates
16301 Quorum Dr., Suite 150-A
Addison, TX 75001
www.BizComPress.com

Read this Disclaimer

CONTENTS

12 Amazing Franchise Opportunities

Amazing Franchise Tools

Introduction

If you already know about franchising and you think it's an amazing concept, you may want to skip the Introduction and head directly into the chapters to read about the amazing franchise opportunities presented in this book. But if you're curious about why I think franchising is amazing, and you want to know more about what's in this book, please continue reading.

The first time a franchisor explained to me how franchising works, I thought the concept was *amazing*. After building a successful business, a franchisor offers (of course, for a fee) to teach others how to operate the same business in a different location or market. *Amazing*...and here's why.

Got an Amazing Idea?

Most people can't come up with a good business idea, let alone know how to build a prototype and successfully open the doors to paying customers. Most people are going to trip up over where to locate the business, or how to negotiate with suppliers, or how to market and advertise the business, or how to charge for products or services, or how to keep customers coming back time after time, or all of that and more.

In other words, most people who start a business are going to fail, and they do. Every year would-be business owners lose billions of dollars in America alone, all because they didn't know what successful franchisors know.

The Secret is in the System

You'll notice that I said "successful franchisors" because not everyone who becomes a franchisor succeeds. But successful franchisors, those who invest the time and the money—especially the money—to build profitable and satisfying businesses also develop a series of systems that they can transfer and teach to other people: franchisees. Everything that successful franchisors know becomes part of a system. And it's the system that franchisees rely on to replicate the franchisor's success.

How does McDonald's eliminate the guesswork about where to open a new unit? That knowledge is part of McDonald's site selection system. How does a McDonald's franchisee know how many hamburger rolls to purchase on any given day, and how many people will be needed to operate the business during an eight-hour shift? The answers are part of McDonald's operating system.

In fact, you can't ask a question that McDonald's, the franchisor, can't answer about how to operate a successful McDonald's restaurant. And now, just imagine, McDonald's is willing to share all of its knowledge with you, or any qualified prospect, to become a franchisee anywhere in the world. Tell me that's not amazing!

You Can Minimize the Risk

What's more amazing, and this is what I thought about the first time a franchisor explained franchising to me, is that I do not have to come up with a good business idea, go into debt to develop the idea in the hopes that it would become a profitable and satisfying business, and then fail. I don't have to take that risk because there are at least 3,000 different franchise opportunities in North America alone. It's easier to find a business concept that I like, and then pay the franchisor to teach me how to operate the business successfully in a new location. Or, I can buy an existing franchise business and bypass the more treacherous start-up years.

I didn't come from a business-minded family, so I knew very little about how to develop and operate a business. And yet, I wanted to own a business because I knew that working for someone else wasn't going to fulfill my expectations. I was never going to make enough money working for someone else, and I'm not a 9-to-5 type of employee.

But until I learned about franchising, I didn't think I could ever own a business. I've since owned several franchises, I've been the CEO of a major franchisor organization, and I've devoted a career to advising franchisors and franchisees, writing about franchising, and teaching people how to take advantage of this amazing concept.

Franchising is an Equalizer

Through the years I've become acquainted with countless people internationally who told me they didn't think they had a chance to own a business because of their circumstances. Some of these people had great ideas for new businesses, but most of them did not have the money to start a business, and many of them did not have a formal education—in fact, several never graduated from high school. No one claimed to know how to build a business.

But once these people discovered franchising most of their doubts and limitations disappeared over time, and they built profitable and satisfying businesses, and in some cases, financial empires.

It's important to know, as successful franchisors and franchisees will tell you, that while franchising levels the playing field so that most everyone can succeed in business, it doesn't suddenly make everything all right. It makes everything possible, at least in terms of developing a successful business, but it doesn't remove all the risks or limitations, and it surely doesn't do the work for you. Many people are fond of saying that franchising is "turnkey," and unfortunately that leads some people to believe that all they have to do is get the key, turn it, and *voila!*, success. But it's not *that* amazing!

Franchising isn't a miraculous solution. I don't know any lazy or uninformed people who have succeeded in franchising. Conversely, of the successful franchisors and franchisees I know, none is a genius. Most are simply hard-working, curious, ambitious people. Some earned college degrees; others did not. Some had family money; most did not. Many struggled before they succeeded, and some failed and started again, but none gave up.

Other than franchising as a common bond, successful franchisors and franchisees also share the ability to be led. Obviously franchisees need to learn how to be successful in business—that's the purpose of the franchisor's system—but franchisors are not infinitely wise; the best of them recognize that they need to be taught and guided, too, and they invest time and money in their continuing educations. Anyone who isn't willing to be led to greater accomplishments isn't cut out for franchising, as amazing as it may be.

But is Franchising for You?

Even if you agree with me that franchising is amazing, you ultimately have to decide if franchising is for you. You may already have decided that it is and that's why you're reading this book, or you may still be searching for answers even while you're searching for an amazing franchise opportunity. Either way, this book can help you make the decision. Because even though the book is devoted to telling you about 12 amazing franchise opportunities, I've also included additional information that will help you not only decide if franchising is for you, but if it is, what type of franchise is best for you.

Here's What's in the Book

In addition, I've included important information about how to buy a franchise opportunity, sharing with you step-by-step instructions for making a good buying decision, including many of the questions you should ask. Check out "17 Steps to Successfully Buying a Franchise." And if you will need money to buy a franchise, I've covered that for you, too. You'll want to read "Funding Your Franchise Acquisition: Where Do You Get The Money?"

And, oh, by the way, if you're not an American citizen, but you want to use your investment in a franchise or in franchising to move to America under the EB-5 Foreign Investor Program, you'll want to read "Use Franchising to Get Your U.S. Green Card."

Franchising Caters to Your Desires

So here's another amazing fact about franchising. There's something for (almost) everyone!

❖ You want to work from home? You can.

❖ You want to work from a truck? You can.

❖ You want to work in a store at the mall or a strip center? You can.

❖ You want to provide a service instead of selling a product? You can.

❖ You want to own multiple units of the same

franchise brand? You can.

❖ You want to own multiple franchise brands? You can.

❖ You want to own a territory in which you sell the franchises and then train and support the franchisees while also owning your own unit? You can.

❖ You want to live the life of an expat building an international franchise empire? You can.

The opportunities are endless. If franchising makes sense for you—and it does not for everyone—then it's a matter of finding the circumstances that make sense for you. And again, that process has been systematized.

Late in the book, following the 12 amazing franchise opportunity stories, I included "Match Your Personality to the Appropriate Franchise Opportunities" to help you discover once and for all not only if franchising is for you, but what kind of franchise makes sense for you. In fact, you might want to jump to that information now because once you know if you're a fit, and how you fit, it's a lot easier to find the right franchise opportunity. And there's a good chance you'll find that opportunity in this book.

Why These 12 Franchise Opportunities?

After I decided to compile this book, and BizCom Press agreed to publish it, we invited franchisors to tell their story in hopes that they might find future franchisees, such as you. I don't think it will come as a surprise to you that this is a matchmaking book designed to help you find an amazing franchise opportunity.

But you might be wondering: Of all the franchise opportunities that exist worldwide, why these 12?

When we invited franchisors to submit their stories, we had two primary qualifications: (1) For logistical purposes we limited the book to 12 stories, so the franchisors had to make the cut into the top 12; and (2) there had to be at least one amazing aspect about the franchise opportunity, and we reserved the right to decide what was amazing. These 12 franchise opportunities qualified because their stories are more amazing than others. Several of them are name brands that you probably already know; others are new, or new to you because you've not seen them in your community or state. And each one is amazing not for one, but for multiple reasons.

So yes, there are other amazing franchise opportunities besides these 12, but these 12 are my choice for 2015. Before each of the 12 stories, I include a brief introduction explaining why I think each franchise opportunity is amazing. If you agree with me when you read the stories, I recommend that you request more information from the franchisors. I've made the process of requesting information easy for you, too; just click on the banner that appears at the end of the 12 chapters and you'll get information via your email.

For now, the only thing left to do is continue reading and find an amazing franchise opportunity that makes sense for you!

November 2014

17 Steps to Successfully Buying a Franchise

Everything is possible with a system!

Outstanding achievements are the results of someone following a system. With the right systems you can succeed at almost anything. What is it that you want? There's a system to help you get it.

You want to successfully buy a franchise? It won't surprise you, I don't think, to discover that there's a system for doing so. And here it is: "17 Steps to Successfully Buying a Franchise." If you follow these guidelines, you're taking all the right steps to explore franchising, to consider the pros and cons of franchising, and, if franchising makes sense for you, to ultimately find a franchise opportunity worthy of your investment.

Even though I cannot guarantee your success as a franchisee—no one can because there are so many variables at play—if you complete these 17 steps you can eventually sign your name to a franchise agreement with the confidence that you've done everything possible to ensure your own success as a franchisee. Of course, you must follow the system and complete each step with integrity.

Based on that understanding, here are the 17 steps to successfully buying a franchise:

Educate Yourself

1. As you prepare to buy a franchise, spend time reading (or viewing informational videos) to make sure you understand what franchising is all about. You can also get good information at franchise conferences and through franchise advisors. One way or another, get familiar with the fundamentals of franchising.

Questions you should ask:

> *Why is franchising so successful?*
>
> *What are the main reasons for franchise failure?*
>
> *How can I be sure that a franchisor is legitimate?*

Why Franchising Exists

2. Of all the points that you need to understand about franchising, the most important may be this: *Franchising is a system of distribution.* Franchising is a means for marketing and selling products and services. Don't get caught up in any of the hype about franchising. Yes, of course, it's a way for you to own your own business, and it may be the safest way to do so, and it may be your ticket to financial independence, but do not overlook the fundamental purpose of franchising: *It's to sell stuff!*

Questions you should ask:

> *Am I excited about distributing the franchisor's products and services?*

Do I see myself operating this system for five, 10, or more years?

How can I be sure that the franchisor's system will work in my territory?

Does Franchising Make Sense for You?

3. Be absolutely sure that franchising makes sense for you. Franchisors are not interested in selling franchises to the wrong prospects or investors. You should be equally as protective of yourself. Ask the question: *Is franchising for me?* Keep in mind that it's not for everyone. If it's not for you, don't force it. Use the personality assessments described at the end of this book to help you learn more about your compatibility with franchises.

Questions you should ask:

What qualifies me to be a franchisee?

Why do I want to be a franchisee?

What type of franchise will make the most sense for me?

Know Your Role as a Franchisee

4. Understand that the franchisor creates the *system* and the franchisees follow the system. Good franchisors know what needs to be done day to day, month to month, to succeed in the business. And that's what they'll expect you to do. Everything you're required to do is part of the system...so you must be willing to follow it, even if you don't always agree with it. Otherwise the franchisor can take away your franchise. The franchise agreement mandates that you follow the franchisor's system.

Questions you should ask:

> *How can I learn more about the franchisor's system?*
>
> *What aspects of the system may or may not be of interest to me?*
>
> *Do existing franchisees endorse the franchisor's system?*

You're Buying a License

5. By legal definition, a franchise is a license. A franchisor licenses a franchisee to operate a specific business in a specific manner at a specific location (or in a specific region) for a specific period of time. The license can be renewed and either party also can terminate it. Be sure you understand those details before you invest.

Furthermore, the franchisor retains ownership of (almost) everything! The franchisor's intellectual property, training materials, marketing methodologies, sales processes, possibly even phone numbers and clients, always remain the property of the franchisor, and not the franchisee. These details will be explained in the Franchise Disclosure Document.

Questions you should ask:

> *What are the specific terms of the franchise agreement?*

> *Do I get a protected territory? (You may not want a protected territory and you do not necessarily need one, depending on the franchise.)*

> *What if I decide I want to sell the franchise; how do I do that?*

The Franchise Work Environment

6. Think about the franchise work environment. Most franchisors require franchisees to be owners/operators. In other words, you can't be an absentee owner. Some franchisors expect franchisees to work from home, or a small office. Other franchisors require franchisees to work from a retail shop at a strip center or a mall. Other franchisors require franchisees to work from a van or another type of vehicle. In some cases franchisees work alone; in other cases franchisees manage employees. Once you know which work environment makes sense for you, pursue franchise opportunities that support your preferences.

Questions you should ask:

> *Do I want to manage people?*

Am I comfortable working alone, from my home or a small office?

If I prefer one work environment but the franchise companies of my choice require a different work environment, can I adjust?

Did You Know They Franchised *That?*

7. There are at least 75 primary industries that use franchising as their method of distribution. Once people explore franchises, they're surprised by the industries that have developed franchise opportunities. It's a good chance that, until you read this book, you did not know there was a franchise in the swimming pool industry, the dental repair industry, the janitorial industry, and the vaping industry, among others. It's best to find the industry that makes sense for you. Keep in mind that from industry to industry, franchise investment costs vary.

Questions you should ask:

Which industries interest me the most?

Which industries can I afford?

Which industries provide me with the best opportunities?

Look for the Right Opportunity

8. No one knows how many franchise opportunities exist, but estimates suggest there are about 3,000 opportunities in North America alone. Many of these opportunities are local or regional, and some of the companies are sold out so they're not offering franchises except internationally. Some industries include a dozen or more franchise companies offering similar and competitive franchise opportunities, while other industries may only include a handful of franchisors. Of course, these numbers are of little consequence considering that you're looking for just one franchise: the one that's best for you. You will find these opportunities by reading books and articles, attending expos, and by being observant: What's being franchised today that interests you?

Questions you should ask:

> *How much money can I invest in a franchise? The answer may dictate the industries that you should explore.*
>
> *How do I want to spend the next five, 10, or more years of my life in business?*
>
> *When it comes to "selling stuff," what excites me?*

Information is Free; Ask for It!

9. When you find a company that interests you, ask for information. It's free, and it comes without any strings attached. Remember, a U.S.-based franchisor must provide

U.S. citizens with a disclosure document at least two weeks before selling a franchise. The clock doesn't begin to tick until you acknowledge receiving the disclosure document. And franchisors will not send you that document until they've had an opportunity to speak with you and know that you are qualified to invest in their business. There's no reason not to ask for information, provided you're genuinely interested in the franchise. You can expect the company to ask you for your personal information before sharing information with you. Generally, a franchisor wants to get your email address, your phone number, the timeframe in which you plan to buy a franchise, and an understanding of how much money you intend to invest in a business. By the way, it's a mistake to provide misleading information—once you're found out, do you think the franchisor will trust you?

Questions you should ask:

Are you planning to open franchises in my territory of choice?

How much is the investment in your franchise?

What makes your franchise business unique and amazing?

Carefully Read the Information

10. Invest time to carefully read the information provided by the franchisor. Make sure you not only can see yourself as a franchisee, but that you understand the business and the requirements of franchisees in your company of choice. The franchisor's preliminary information may not be specific, but the information in the franchisor's disclosure document must be specific. If you like what you're reading (perhaps even seeing, if the franchisor provides links to videos) plan to ask for the disclosure document.

Questions you should ask:

> *If I were to invest in this franchise, what else would I need to know?*
>
> *Is this a business that makes sense for my location, or territory?*
>
> *Where's this business headed in the next five to 10 years?*

Attend the Franchisor's Discovery Day

11. Visit the franchisor. Almost every franchisor sponsors a Discovery Day. This is your chance to visit the franchisor's headquarters, meet company representatives, possibly even franchisees, and learn more about the franchise opportunity by listening to a variety of presentations and asking questions. The franchisor may also include a tour to show you the training center, the marketing department, etc. Franchisors do not charge a fee for Discovery Days, but you most likely will be expected to provide your own transportation and lodging. However, don't be afraid to ask the franchisor to pay for your expenses, or to share your expenses. Depending on how eager the franchisor is to sell a franchise, you may get a free trip. But even if you have to shell out some money for this experience, it's worth it. If you're married, the franchisor may want your spouse to attend, too.

Questions you should ask:

How is this business unique and amazing?

How does this business compare to similar franchises?

What's the future for this industry, and this franchise in particular?

Get Disclosed

12. Ask the franchisor for the Franchise Disclosure Document (FDD). Once the franchisor knows that you're a "serious" candidate to buy a franchise, by law the franchisor must "disclose" you before continuing to talk to you about the franchise opportunity. This is a very serious matter and franchisors are careful not to violate it.

When you ask for the disclosure document the franchisor will ask you for detailed information to qualify your candidacy. Be prepared to tell the franchisor about your net worth, your personal and professional background (including any criminal violations), and the timeframe in which you plan to buy a franchise. Expect the franchisor to investigate this information by running a credit history and a criminal background check. The franchisor may also require you to complete a franchise personality assessment.

Receiving a FDD does not obligate you to do anything! You must have this document for at least 14 days prior to buying the franchise. But you're not obligated until you sign the franchise agreement.

Questions you should ask:

> *How long has this franchise been in business; who owns it; how are the franchise company's executives qualified to be in their positions?*

> *How much training and support will I receive? Does it cost extra money?*

> *How often (if ever) have franchisees sued the franchisor, and why?*

Go to Work for a Franchisee

13. One of the most important steps you can take before buying a franchise is to talk to existing franchisees. Call them, visit them, and spend time with them. The FDD includes a list of existing and former franchisees—use that list; it's one of the most important tools for franchise exploration.

Existing franchisees will talk to you by phone, or if they're in close proximity to you, they may invite you for a personal meeting. Some franchisees may not be willing to talk to you at all, but most franchisees remember what it was like when they were exploring franchise opportunities, and they're willing to help you because someone once helped them. Franchisees also realize that it's important for their franchise networks to expand—it gives them greater visibility in the marketplace (more franchisees means more money in the national advertising fund), and greater clout when negotiating with suppliers.

Here's an idea that you will find extremely helpful: Go to work for an existing franchisee. Offer to work weekends, or part time, for a month or more to experience the franchise operation. This is a practical way for you to discover your interest in a specific business. Many franchisors will require that you at least meet with an existing franchisee to discuss your prospects for joining the franchise network.

"Are franchisees getting paid to tell me good things so that I'll buy the franchise?" If they are, the information will be revealed in the FDD, or the franchisor is violating federal laws in the U.S.! Generally, franchisors do not pay franchisees for speaking to prospective franchisees. However, franchisors sometimes sponsor competitions, i.e. the franchisee that helps sell the most franchises in a year receives $10,000! But that information also must be disclosed in the FDD.

Questions you should ask:

Would you buy this same franchise again?

What are the franchisor's greatest strengths...
  weaknesses?

*How much money can I expect to earn after a
year as a franchisee? After three years?*

Decide if You Can Afford the Investment

14. Study Item 7 of the franchisor's FDD to understand
your financial commitment when you buy this franchise.
Federal law requires U.S. franchisors to clearly disclose financial information in the FDD. Item 7, Estimated Initial Investment, presents each financial commitment in a chart
that shows you when the money is due to be paid, to whom it
must be paid (i.e. the franchisor, a media company, a landlord, or a supplier), and whether or not the money is refundable. This is the best way to see the required financial commitment at a glance.

Keep in mind that the franchisor must include every financial requirement in Item 7, which eliminates surprises.
"Oh, we didn't tell you that you owe $5,000 for training?"
That sort of thing doesn't happen anymore in franchising.

Questions you should ask:

Can I afford to invest this amount of money?

*Do existing franchisees say that the investment is
reasonable?*

*How does this financial commitment compare to
investments in competitive opportunities?*

Understand the Ongoing Fees

15. Look at the ongoing royalty and advertising fee requirements, which are not part of Item 7. Most franchisors require franchisees to pay a percentage of gross sales as a royalty every month—the percentage may be as low as five percent and as high as twelve percent, and varies from company to company. The advertising fee is also a percentage of gross sales and may be in the range of one percent to three percent paid monthly.

Questions you should ask:

Do the royalty and advertising fees seem reasonable?

How does the franchisor spend the royalty dollars paid by franchisees?

Is the national advertising fund effective for boosting retail sales?

Get Help!

16. Consult with your professional advisors. You should spend the money to engage a franchise attorney and an accountant prior to signing a franchise agreement. There are many franchise attorneys at work in the U.S. and other countries and you can find them through a franchise association such as the International Franchise Association (www.franchise.org). You will likely pay $500 to $1,500 for the attorney's basic services. You will likely pay more money to an attorney who does not specialize in franchise law—that's like asking your franchise attorney to handle a personal injury suit. If an attorney suggests he/she negotiate with the franchisor on your behalf, be very careful. Franchisors rarely negotiate and franchise attorneys know that. However, franchise attorneys also know areas in which a franchisor is likely to negotiate and may be helpful in that regard.

It's more difficult to find an accountant who is familiar with franchising and who understands franchising. Too often accountants are anti-franchising and they advise their clients to start businesses independently rather than to join a franchise network and pay fees. That's unfortunate because statistics demonstrate that in many industries franchises are more successful than independently owned businesses. My best advice for finding a "franchise friendly" accountant is to find an accountant who is also a franchisee! In other words, the accountant's practice is part of a franchise network. Again, you can find these businesses through franchise associations. A good accountant will be able to help you develop a business plan and assess your financial risk as well as rewards. Accounting fees vary widely, but for basic services expect to pay $500 to $1,500. Keep in mind that you also may need an accountant after you become a franchisee to prepare your quarterly and annual statements.

Keep in mind that professional advisors are not supposed to make decisions for you. "Should I buy this franchise?" is a question that a good advisor will not answer. Advisors will point out pros and cons; ultimately, you make the decisions.

Other possible advisors include franchise brokers and coaches. When you engage these advisors, make certain that you understand what's in it for them. Brokers sell franchises for a living; they do not advise franchise prospects except as part of their mission to sell a franchise. Brokers generally do not charge fees to their clients because the franchisor pays them when they sell a franchise. There's nothing wrong with this arrangement, by the way, and franchisors that rely on brokers must reveal this information in the FDD.

Questions you should ask:

> *How does this franchise opportunity compare to others you've reviewed?*
>
> *What are the problem areas that you see investing in this type of franchise?*
>
> *Based on my financial situation, is this a franchise I can afford?*

Make Your Final Decision

17. Take a deep breath, offer up any final prayers, and say "yes" to the franchisor of your choice. Go ahead; sign the franchise agreement. Congratulations, you're a franchisee! If you did your homework, and followed the recommendations offered to you in this book and through other sources, you're on your way to stardom!

Questions you should ask:

When does my training session begin?

What three things must I be sure to do to succeed in this business?

What three things must I be sure not to do to succeed in this business?

When I'm buying a franchise, and when I coach my clients who are buying franchises, I use these 17 steps to success. Each step includes multiple tasks, and it's important to take the time to complete each step. If you have questions about how to complete these steps, or you need additional guidance, visit my blog at www.HowToBuyAFranchise.com and contact me.

Funding Your Franchise Acquisition:
Where Do You Get the Money?

Two common mistakes that prospective franchisees make when they're exploring franchise opportunities are (1) ignorance of their personal, financial status and capabilities; and (2) ignorance of the financial requirements to buy a franchise.

Do you know your credit score, and how much cash you can invest in a franchise, or bring to the table to leverage additional funds? Do you know what banks, leasing companies, the U.S. Small Business Administration, and special funds designated for franchise lending will require of you to secure a loan?

The sooner you get on top of these issues the better—otherwise, you may be wasting your time. You should expect franchisors, and franchise brokers, to ask you these questions even before they give you a franchise disclosure document. Not to do so could mean the franchisor is wasting his or her time because you may not be able to acquire the franchise.

Good News for Borrowers

If you need to borrow money to acquire a franchise, the good news is that for the first time in many years you have multiple options available. While it was nearly impossible to borrow money to start a franchise between 2008 and 2010, opportunities are more plentiful today, but still not what they were prior to the Great Recession.

While there's still not a national lender for franchise opportunities, as existed prior to 2008, nowadays more community banks lend to franchisees, more franchisors lend to franchisees (you can read about several of them in this eBook), several franchise-specific funds underwrite franchise acquisitions, and for those who have a retirement fund, the fund can be rolled into seed money to capitalize a business.

"Compared to what it was like before the recession, funding franchises is still difficult," explains Bob Coleman, editor of the Coleman Report (www.ColemanReport.com), which provides information to bankers to help them make less risky small business loans. "Lenders are scrutinizing deals and are particularly interested in the performance of the brand, something that didn't matter as much previously."

Not Good News for New Brands

"Unless a franchisor has 80 to 100 units, there's no deal," continues Coleman. "A start-up brand and a new franchisee is not a favorable combination. Lenders want to see track records by both the brand and the franchisee. Lenders today know about unhappy franchisees and how to check for them, whereas five years ago they didn't care—(pay) 30 percent (money) down and you'd get the loan, but that doesn't happen anymore."

According to Coleman, lenders view franchises as "a little bit better risk than mom-and-pop businesses," but they're insisting on funding deals for established brands. They also prefer experienced franchisees. "If you've been successfully operating a unit for several years and now you need money to open another one to three units, you can get that money."

Franchising is Growing Once Again

As the economy continues to grow, lenders are becoming more receptive to franchise deals, and franchise companies are growing, too. In fact, Frandata, the franchise information firm based outside of Washington, D.C., reported that franchising is now growing at its fastest rate in five years, largely because prospective and existing franchisees have been able to find money.

Frandata said demand for franchise units would increase by more than 12 percent in 2014, the highest rate since 2009, and predicted that franchising's lending shortfall, defined as the difference between loan demand and loan supply, would be cut in half before 2015. Meanwhile, in 2014, the franchise sector created more than 220,000 new jobs. In general, franchise businesses add employees at a rate faster than the national economy, and of small businesses.

According to Frandata, demand for new and existing franchisees in 2014 was expected to exceed 73,800 units, a 12.4 percent increase over 2013, and an 18.8 percent increase over 2012. To satisfy that demand, franchises would need $29.4 billion in loans. Banks are expected to make $28.1 billion available, funding 70,500 units. That's a 4.4-percent gap, easily the smallest since the numbers have been tracked. In 2010, the gap was 16.6 percent, and it has fallen every year since.

How Do You Get a Loan Today?

So what's it going to take today to get the money you need to acquire a franchise opportunity?

Business financing expert, Doug Smith of Biz Finance Solutions in Colorado (www.BizFinanceSolutions.com), explains that there are two types of funding: equity-based, and debt-based.

"Using the money you have in your retirement plan, rolling it over without penalty or taxation, and using it as an injection to get a U.S. government-backed loan, is equity financing," he says, and it's an option that many franchisees use today.

"Debt-based funding requires a credit score and credit history to get a conventional bank loan or unsecured business financing, including equipment leasing, and unsecured personal loans. But if your credit score is weak, or you've filed a bankruptcy, it's the kiss of death."

Your personal financial situation, and your thoughts about financial risk, may determine how you should proceed when you seek financing.

The 401k Rollover

Smith's preferred franchise funding strategy is the 401k Rollover (tinyurl.com/mteb5ds), and most people don't seem to know about it. Or if they do, they've been told it's illegal or dangerous. However, this option has the blessing of the U.S. government, and here are the facts you need to know:

If you have a retirement fund and you change employers, you have three important options:

1. Leave the fund where it is...the majority of people choose this option.

2. Move the fund into a new account, such as a self-directed IRA.

3. Move the fund to your new employer's 401k, thus consolidating your retirement savings in one fund.

Most people aren't aware of Option #3, beginning with becoming your own employer!

That is, you can become a franchisee and establish a C Corporation (tinyurl.com/k8n7dqp) with stock and a 401k. Becoming your own employer puts you in the enviable position of self-funding your own business, tax-free! You can move—or what the Internal Revenue Service refers to as roll-over—your existing retirement money into your new employer's 401k, and the cash can be used to buy and operate a franchise. It's tax-free, penalty-free (if done correctly), it's legal (www.irs.gov/taxtopics/tc424.html), and it may be your best option for funding your business, particularly if you don't have other resources, or you can't qualify for a traditional loan.

Isn't This Controversial?

The U.S. Internal Revenue Service, and the Department of Labor, have established guidelines and directives for implementing a 401k Rollover. You can't use the rollover to dodge taxes, or to personally benefit from the money. Some years ago a financial broker was shut down for a period of time for stretching the rules, and that incident gave rise to the notion that the rollover is illegal. It's not. If you use the rollover for the right reasons—you can't use it for a scheme; it has to be used with a real business—you (or your advisor) set it up correctly, and comply annually with the regulations, you should be able to avoid any objections or complications. Follow the spirit of the guidelines with appropriate intentions and you should remain in the clear.

Of course, the IRS reserves the right to change the rules, and that's why it's extremely important that you work with a credible company, or broker, that has a track record for successfully implementing and maintaining rollovers.

Two Benefits of a 401k Rollover

The 401k Rollover has made a good name for itself among franchisors, who frequently recommend the strategy to prospective franchisees. Here are two reasons why:

❖ If the franchise acquisition is a small investment— under $150,000—franchisors know that lenders aren't attracted to small loans. There's no money to be made processing small loans, so lenders avoid them. That makes a rollover more attractive. Rollover money can be used to pay for the franchise fee, and to buy equipment. When you don't have collateral, or you're buying a business that provides a service from your home, a vehicle, or a small office, the 401k Rollover may be your best choice for funding your business.

❖ After a rollover, you can use the cash as equity to qualify for a conventional or SBA-guaranteed loan. You'll likely need a cash injection of 30 percent to secure a loan. In the past, borrowers used equity in real estate, i.e. their personal residence, to qualify for a loan. Now you can use rollover money for your cash injection.

"People who utilize a rollover are more successful in the average business," reveals Geoff Seiber, president and CEO of FranFund in Fort Worth, Texas (www.FranFund.com). "People who use this strategy tend to stay in business longer because they used their retirement money to fund their business and they don't have debt to service."

Can You Accept the Risks?

Used properly, the 401k Rollover is an aggressive way to capitalize your business. The challenge, however, is that by using it you give up the security of a retirement fund. Some people can't handle that emotionally. *Can you?* Will you feel comfortable knowing that your retirement money is now invested in your own business? If not, you probably don't want to use this funding strategy. On the other hand, people who start businesses, and plan to operate them, aren't usually looking for comfort.

In the U.S., numerous companies provide rollover services, including: Biz Finance Solutions, Guidant, FranFund, and Benetrends. Expect to spend in the range of $5,000 with one of these firms to set up your rollover. The firm will also offer to provide necessary administrative services to keep your fund in check, and that may cost you in the range of $100 monthly.

It's important to keep your rollover plan in compliance with the laws because the IRS audits these plans. "Under two percent of our plans are audited every year," says Seiber, "which is the norm in our industry. By not doing the administrative work properly you're taking a bigger risk" if the IRS audits your account.

Options to the 401k Rollover

Unless you have a pile of cash that you intend to inject into your deal, i.e. a retirement fund that you will rollover, or savings that you will bring to the table, your funding options are severely limited. It's even worse if you're a new franchisee and you want to buy a single unit—an existing franchisee with plans to expand, or a multi-unit operator, will find more options.

As a result of the recession, many franchisors realized that if they wanted to sell franchises, they'd have to share the risk with franchisees and possibly third-party lenders. This created an opportunity for companies such as Franchise Loans Direct (FLD; tinyurl.com/plnwg9s) to offer financing, but almost exclusively to franchisees of established brands.

Bob Rodi administers the FLD program through a non-bank funding platform "We manage origination, underwriting, documentation and funding of franchise loans in the $100,000 to $5 million range in 50 states and U.S. territories," he explains.

Food and Service Brands are Popular

Most of FLD's loans go to franchisees who select food brands, but several service brands also have qualified for the program. "We are very picky about the franchise companies that we approve for FLD," says Rodi, "because our only collateral in this program is the franchise business itself and personal guarantees from the principals. The franchisor's background, reputation and track record for making franchisees successful is extremely important to us."

Even though single-unit buyers are not his target market, Rodi says he'll help those buyers, if he can, by directing them to pursue an SBA-backed loan at a bank where they will get the lowest interest rate, which is in the range of six to eight percent. However, conventional bank loans require collateral, so buyers need to pledge assets to secure the loan. That's not the best option, but it may be the only option for many buyers. Rodi's willing to help these buyers because down the road, when they're ready to expand, he may be able to replace their SBA loan. "We'll take these buyers out of the SBA loan to grow multiple stores," he explains.

"Someone who's buying five units of a brand," which is Rodi's target market, "won't have a problem with our higher interest rate, which is 9.9 percent," he says. "The multi-unit operator who has business acumen understands leveraging assets rather than pledging assets, which you don't do with us."

Look to Your Franchisor for Funding

Guys like Rodi, Coleman, Smith, and Seiber are among a select corps of experts who can advise prospective franchisees when they need financing, but there's only so much they can do in a reticent financial market. If you can't take advantage of the programs they offer or recommend, your best source of funding may be your franchisor of choice. If you know that you will need money to acquire a franchise, look for franchisors that lend to franchisees, beginning with several in this eBook. Even franchisors that don't loan money to franchisees know who will, and what's required, so ask your finance related questions early in your franchise exploration.

And don't give up! Some of the most successful franchisees today started out by investing in a low-cost franchise and expanding when they could afford to do so. Many others started out with money borrowed from family and friends. If franchising makes sense for you, you'll find a franchise company that will help you clear the lending hurdles.

Here's One More Funding Option: VetFran®

VetFran, sponsored by the International Franchise Association (IFA), helps veterans of the U.S. armed services buy franchise opportunities by providing financial assistance, training, and industry support.

VetFran was created by the late Don Dwyer Sr.—founder of The Dwyer Group, a conglomerate of franchise companies, to say "thank you" to America's veterans returning from the first Gulf War. After the Sept. 11, 2001 terrorist attacks, IFA re-launched VetFran and the program continues to this day.

Nearly 600 franchise brands, including the 12 in this eBook, voluntarily offer financial incentives and mentoring to prospective franchisees who are veterans. Thousands of veterans have utilized VetFran to buy franchises. If you're a veteran, be sure to ask your franchisor of choice, "Do you support VetFran?" This may be an additional source of funding for you.

12 Amazing

Franchise Opportunities

Always Fast, Always Fresh, Always Friendly

What do consumers want to buy every day? Convenience! And here's a franchise company that sells it without consumers ever needing to get out of their vehicles. Farm Stores, a 50-year-old company that's never been franchised, but operates 70 some stores in Florida, is now offering area development licenses and individual units to qualified prospects nationally and internationally.

This is an amazing ground floor opportunity!

Farm Stores is a drive-thru convenience store that offers consumers the most popular items needed daily (and often at the last minute)...milk, eggs, beverages, cleaning supplies, baked goods, wine and nearly 200 other name brand products.

Through years of development, Farm Stores has created an experience that brings loyal customers back to the store every week and sometimes every day. Top shoppers spend at least $10 per visit and again, never get out of their vehicles.

Farm Stores serves them while they wait, and the wait is never long.

The franchisor offers nationwide distribution, a unique local marketing program, comprehensive training and support, and research and development to meet future consumer needs. Investment costs are reasonable, and you'll be surprised to learn how many employees it takes to staff a store.

This is a $700 billion industry that's targeted for growth in the U.S. and many other countries. Farm Stores invites multi-unit ownership. Read the details and ask for more information today.

—Dr. John P. Hayes

Franchise and Area Development Opportunities Coming to Your Neighborhood

Nothing's more important to shoppers than convenience, especially when they're in a hurry, and nothing's more convenient than a drive-thru store that offers 200-plus popular items ranging from milk and eggs to wine and fresh baked bread.

And no one knows this better than Farm Stores, which for the first time in its 50-plus year history is offering franchises and area development licenses for its convenience stores to qualified entrepreneurs nationally and internationally.

"Our number one selling point to consumers is convenience," says Chief Operating Officer Maurice Bared, "but our number one selling point to franchisees is the ability to grow their business through multi-unit ownership or by taking advantage of our area developer opportunities. Area developers within a specific territory by agreement award franchises; then they assist those new franchisees in the training, operations, support, supply and compliance of our system. Convenience stores are a well-known concept and they are popular franchise opportunities," continues Bared, "but this one comes with a drive-thru, and more than five decades of success. Everyone thinks this is an amazing opportunity."

There's never a need to get out of your vehicle at Farm Stores.

Greater Demand for Convenience

Time-starved consumers value convenience stores because they offer neighborhood locations, extended hours of operation, one-stop shopping, a variety of merchandise, and fast transactions. Farm Stores' shoppers get all that without leaving their vehicles! Industry experts project that sales revenues will continue increasing in the convenience store sector for at least the next five years because consumers are enjoying more personal disposable income, which creates even greater demand for convenience.

Customers depend on Farm Stores to deliver products to their vehicle.

Founded in Miami, Florida, Farm Stores' drive-thru outlets were created to save shoppers time, but also to meet the needs of a burgeoning market that exists almost everywhere today. "Two-thirds of our customers are women," says Bared, who joined the company in 1994 and became COO in 1998, "and in addition to convenience, they value safety. When they come to the Farm Stores and it's raining, snowing, or the sun's beating down hot, or if they've got children in the car, it's another huge benefit that they can stay in their vehicle and let the Farm Stores' staff go to work on their behalf. We gather their products, process their payment, deliver to their car, and send them on their way."

Better Margins for Convenience and Brand

Another huge benefit is being able to buy the most popular items that every household seems to need at the last minute. When Farms Stores is in the neighborhood, no one drives to the supermarket to buy diapers, ketchup, hot dog rolls, or fresh baked goods. And no one balks at paying a little more for the opportunity to save time. Besides, the products are the dominant brand and size that everyone wants.

Farm Stores knows its customers, and by creating an experience that meets their customers' needs, the great majority of customers return to the stores every week and sometimes every day. Top shoppers spend at least $10 per visit. The Farm Stores' customer is a loyal customer, and that's a critical accomplishment that doesn't occur by chance. Farm Stores intended it that way. "Our slogan is 'always fast, always fresh, and always friendly,' " says Bared, who spends much of his time focused on improving the development, product line, training and service provided by Farm Stores.

An Operating System for Franchisees

Farm Stores also has created an experience that meets the desires and needs of franchisees. Of its 70-plus store network, the franchisor operates 13 units, so the franchisor knows precisely how to develop and execute a successful business. Nothing in the franchisee's experience is left to chance.

Branded products are popular sales items at Farm Stores.

To wit, the franchisor's turnkey program resolves the critical issues that would likely prevent the success of an independent owner/operator who wasn't part of a franchise network. Here are several examples of what the franchisor provides to guide and support franchisees:

55

❖ **Nationwide distribution.** "We can open a store anywhere in the U.S. and several other countries and our distributor will provide branded merchandise and food products," explains Bared. "It's a huge benefit to franchisees that Farm Stores uses its network's ever growing buying power to negotiate prices for distribution. That spares the franchisee from a decision that ultimately impacts a store's financial performance." Distribution includes exclusive, high quality Farm Store branded products such as bread, milk, butter, ice cream, and more— anyone for eggnog?

❖ **A unique, local marketing program.** "We are combining social media with the customer's mobile number to solidify a relationship for ongoing and added sales," says Bared. "Our developing program will allow our customers to pre-order to speed up service. Our POS system tracks individual customers as well as what and when they buy, and our marketing targets and builds a customer relationship based on current data knowledge. For example, if we discover that a customer buys coffee and a donut every day between 7 and 8 a.m., we can target an offer to get that same customer to buy complementary products, or to return to the store between 5 and 6 p.m. Or we can invite him for a special discount on Thursdays, for example, or remind him of potential or earned rewards. At all times the customer accrues points for his purchase volume, so he knows the more he buys the bigger his reward. Again, the franchisee doesn't have to worry about how to market the store; we've got it covered."

❖ **Comprehensive training and support.** "Because we are store operators, we know what a franchisee needs to be doing every hour of the day," reveals the COO. "The focus is always on exceeding the customer's expectations. Some hours are busier than others, and during the slower hours, the operator changes the store to get ready for the next burst of activity. Based on history, and our purchase tracking system, we know how many customers to expect every day, when to expect them, and what they're going to buy when they arrive. That is valuable information to a franchisee. Plus, it takes away the challenge of selling products. Our customers don't want to be sold. They know what they want to buy; the franchisee has to be ready to provide it."

❖ **Research & Development.** While Farm Stores are open daily, usually from 7 a.m. to 11 p.m., the stores are currently the busiest from mid-afternoon to early evening. To increase traffic during other day parts, Farm Stores is adding specialty food service products including coffees, soft serve ice cream, gourmet soups, sandwiches, salads, and smoothies. "We continuously research additional opportunities for

increasing store revenues and margins," says Bared, "so this is another operational issue that our franchisees do not have to worry about, but we graciously accept their suggestions."
Emphasis is on developing new product lines with minimal labor requirements. Soft serve ice cream and coffee, for example, are produced by "incredibly efficient machines" that provide quality while reducing labor costs.

Multi-Unit Ownership Invited

With so many products, and multiple customers at any given time, you may be wondering how many employees are needed to operate a Farm Stores unit. You might be surprised to know that it's only two employees per shift. The franchisor's streamlined operating system has reduced the need for labor. "Franchisees can work as employees if they choose to," says Bared, "but it's not a requirement." In fact, Farm Stores encourages multi-unit ownership.

A Store in Every Neighborhood

As Farm Stores rolls out its franchise and area development program, the goal is to open a unit "in every neighborhood of every city to meet the demands of today's world." The word "world" is intentional. "This is an international area development opportunity," explains Bared. "While most of our immediate development will occur in the United States, consumers everywhere are looking for convenience, safety, and brand names, so we'll go where there's demand."

A Popular Franchise Opportunity

There are more than 151,000 convenience stores in the U.S.; accounting for more than $700 billion in annual sales, reports NACS, a national association for convenience retailing. Individual operators own nearly 63 percent of convenience stores, demonstrating the popularity of these stores among entrepreneurs, and others who choose to own their own business. As populations continue to expand, the number of convenience stores will expand not only in America, but in other countries, thus creating new ownership opportunities. "Growth and expansion are perfect reasons for Farm Stores to be selling area development licensing opportunities internationally," explains Bared. He also notes that the low required investment complements the concept's popularity.

In the U.S. the total investment for a Farm Stores franchise, including fixtures, signage, land lease, and equipment, is approximately $300,000, including a $25,000 franchise fee. Investment for area development opportunities is determined based on the territory, which will usually support at least 50 units. "Our investment is about 30 percent of what it would cost to open a store for one of our competitors," Bared explains, "because we can operate from pre-fabricated buildings and typically operate under land leases. We also do not necessarily need a corner location, but a good location that provides easy access for drive-thru customers." Of course, Farm Stores uses its real estate knowledge and competence to assist franchisees in finding the right location.

Farm Stores are popular for fresh products and fast service selling quality brands in a friendly, safe environment. Sounds a lot like the corner grocery store of years gone by. Except this store comes with a convenient drive-thru that benefits both consumers and franchise operators.

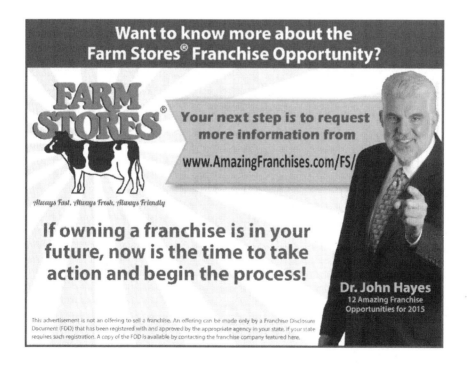

EXPERT APPLIANCE REPAIR

H ere's what you'll find amazing about Mr. Appliance:

❖ Franchisees manage the business;

❖ Technicians provide the service;

❖ The business model is highly predictive based on years of experience;

❖ The brand is very popular in North America;

❖ It's the largest franchised, appliance service business in North America; and

❖ The business is supported by leading edge technology.

In addition, Mr. Appliance is owned by The Dwyer Group, a franchise conglomerate that's existed since the early 1980s. The company was founded by the late Don Dwyer, Sr., who I had the privilege of knowing and serving for many years. Without doubt, Mr. Dwyer was one of the world's most fascinating franchise professionals. He had tremendous vision, and he loved transforming individuals into successful franchisees. "I don't see you for what you are," he would tell franchisees, employees, and vendors, "but for what you can become."

Even though Mr. Dwyer has been gone for many years, his attitudes and beliefs prevail, and The Dwyer Group is widely considered one of the world's most successful franchise networks specializing in home-service businesses.

Today's homes rely on more appliances than ever, including refrigerators, stoves/ovens, dishwashers, dryers, washing machines, microwaves, freezers, trash compactors, etc. An opportunity is created each time one of these appliances fails because consumers have learned to depend on their appliances and they refuse to live without them. So appliance repair is a necessary and repetitive business which will continue to expand.

And who will consumers call when their appliances need to be repaired? Mr. Appliance, of course. It's the perfect opportunity for building a predictable, amazing business.

—Dr. John P. Hayes

Your Business Ownership Dream Starts with Mr. Appliance

Appliance servicing and repair is a needed and repetitive service in a highly fragmented industry. With Mr. Appliance...

❖ You manage the business; your technicians provide the service.

❖ The business model is highly predictive based on years of experience.

❖ Your business has strong brand recognition as North America's largest franchised appliance servicing business.

❖ You get the benefit of a customer experience model supported by leading edge technology.

The Appliance Servicing Industry

You may have never given the appliance serving industry much thought. In fact, it's one of those industries that most people don't think about until they need an appliance serviced or repaired. Think about the appliance servicing industry for a moment from a business opportunity perspective. With the exception of Mr. Appliance, appliance repair is dominated by small mom-and-pop shops with highly variable customer service levels and with little name recognition or branding.

Now consider the appliance marketplace. Today's homes are packed with more appliances than ever before...a total investment of thousands of dollars. Breaking the opportunity down, consider the average middle-class homeowner, who may have a refrigerator, stove/oven, dishwasher, dryer, washing machine, microwave, freezer, and a trash compactor. That's at least eight appliances in a home. Opportunity is created each time one of these appliances fails because consumers have learned to depend on their appliances and are not willing to live without them. They will repair or replace them when they fail, but the cost of repair is generally a fraction of the cost of replacement.

In addition to the residential marketplace, think about the commercial needs for appliance servicing and repair. Restaurants are a perfect example of an appliance-intensive business that requires their appliances to be operating at maximum efficiency with minimum downtime. Some examples of other appliance-intensive businesses are apartment buildings, rent-to-own companies, and laundromats.

Whether it's the residential or commercial market, appliance repair is a needed and repetitive service. It's not seasonal; it's not cyclical...it's just consistent. It's perfect for building a very predictable, amazing business.

"The industry is strong," comments Mr. Appliance franchisee Scott Stewart. "You can cut back on your discretionary services, but appliances are becoming less of a convenience and more of a necessity. People are doing more things at home, and they really can't afford to have a broken appliance."

Work on your business, not in your business.

Mr. Appliance: The Leader in Appliance Servicing

If the repetitive nature of the residential and commercial demand appeals to you, as well as the idea that industry competition is fragmented at best, then consider Mr. Appliance.

Mr. Appliance is North America's largest appliance repair franchise organization. Since 1996, Mr. Appliance has been helping entrepreneurs build better businesses so they can achieve their personal goals. With over 170 locations, Mr. Appliance has built national name-brand recognition. In addition, the size of Mr. Appliance has allowed for the development and creation of many and varied resources to support the success of each franchisee. What Mr. Appliance has built would take many, many years and hundreds of thousands of dollars to replicate.

The systems at Mr. Appliance are built with both customer and business owner in mind. The foundation is a state-of-the-art, integrated technology platform that allows the business owner to track and measure nearly everything, from marketing, to scheduling and job routing, to inventory, job costs and profitability. And, it all feeds the accounting software for the development of financial statements.

Customers at Mr. Appliance are wowed by their experience from start to finish. They are able to schedule appointments online 24/7 when it's convenient for them. Pricing is provided on the franchisee's iPad before the work begins with profit margins built in. Payment can be made on the iPad with the receipt landing in the customer's email before the technician leaves the property. The customer experience is like no other in the industry, generating significant referral and repeat business.

Mr. Appliance's success has been recognized by *Entrepreneur* magazine's Franchise 500 for three consecutive years. In addition, Mr. Appliance is a Military Friendly Franchise and is rated as Best for Vets. Speaking of veterans, Mr. Appliance offers a 25 percent discount on the minimum initial franchise fee for honorably discharged veterans. As part of a new program, Mr. Appliance is also offering a 20 percent discount on the minimum initial franchise fee for individuals who have served full time in either law enforcement or firefighting for at least two years.

"When it comes to Mr. Appliance, the only competition we have are our own goals, and with Mr. Appliance we have a team of people helping us achieve those goals," say Steven and Tammy Johnson, owners of the Over the Mountain Mr. Appliance in Alabama.

Highly Predictive Business Model

Each component of the business process, from creating market awareness to delivering superior customer service, has been monitored and analyzed to create a very detailed and predictable business model. As a Mr. Appliance business owner, you are provided with the metrics to effectively manage all aspects of your business. You not only have a wealth of information about your business at your fingertips, but you also have valuable benchmark data that you can use for comparative purposes, allowing you to clearly see areas for improvement.

"The technology is light years ahead of everyone else in the industry," says Matt Sarkela, a Mr. Appliance franchisee. "When you get into franchising, it adds a level of professionalism and credibility to your customers. It's easier to track what your business is doing so you can have more control over pricing, inventory and what your techs are doing."

Franchisees Manage the Business; Technicians Provide the Service

Mr. Appliance recognizes that franchisees come from many and varied backgrounds. Some have strong technical experience and others have significant business experience with little technical background. Mr. Appliance's systems have been constructed around best practices and are designed for success regardless of the franchisee's background.

Specific areas of support that Mr. Appliance provides to franchisees include:

❖ **Marketing.** Through target marketing and a strong national brand, Mr. Appliance helps franchisees find high-quality customers. Marketing support includes social media, local search engine optimization and professional marketing materials. In addition, Mr. Appliance is part of The Dwyer Group, which includes other service powerhouses such as: Mr. Rooter, Glass Doctor, Mr. Electric, Aire Serv, The Grounds Guys and Rainbow International. The Dwyer Group facilitates cross-marketing programs to share leads between the seven brands.

❖ **Operations.** Mr. Appliance's team of experienced franchise consultants work closely with each franchisee to get the maximum value out of each of the systems.

❖ **Management.** Mr. Appliance teaches and shares various management and best practices in many areas, including: recruiting, hiring, compensation and retention.

❖ **Finance.** Franchisees have access to detailed statistics and financial reports for their businesses, as well as industry averages for comparison purposes.

❖ **Technical.** Mr. Appliance provides many opportunities for franchisees and their employees to sharpen their skills. Training occurs in many forms: face-to-face (local, regional, national), online and from other franchisees in the network.

You manage the business. Your
technicians provide the service.

❖ **Vendor Discounts.** Because of the collective
purchasing power of the Mr. Appliance system, as
well as the family of Dwyer Group brands, Mr.
Appliance franchisees enjoy significant savings
on many products and services needed to run
their businesses.

Mr. Appliance franchisee Steven Johnson sums up the
Mr. Appliance experience, "Mr. Appliance understands the
market. They know exactly how to help you succeed in the
industry."

Build a Business that has Value

Many business owners work a lifetime building a business around them, and find out too late that it has little market value without their involvement. Mr. Appliance is focused on helping you build a business that is system-based, and does not require you to be there for it to be successful. This type of business has much higher value in the marketplace when you're ready to exit. In addition, Mr. Appliance has a resale department to assist you in finding a buyer for your business when you are ready.

Southern cooking is amazing, don't you agree? And there's no place like Dickey's Barbecue Pit for great southern-style foods.

Now, with the success of Dickey's franchise network, consumers across America enjoy a variety of barbecued meats and tasty side dishes. And for the first time the company is expanding internationally.

Dickey's is a family-inspired business dating back to 1941 when World War I veteran, Travis Dickey, opened the first Dickey's in Dallas, Texas, where the company is still headquartered.

With 500 locations in 43 states by the end of 2014, and another 150 locations in development, barbecue has proven to be a smokin' hot franchise opportunity. Technomic named Dickey's Barbecue Pit the nation's fastest growing restaurant chain, and QSR magazine named the company the Best Franchise Deal. Nation's Restaurant News identified Dickey's as a Top Five Growth chain.

One of Dickey's secrets dates back to Travis Dickey: Attention to detail keeps customers coming back time after time. The same secret also attracts prospective franchisees.

What's amazing about Dickey's? How about the lowest start-up costs for a comparable business in the U.S.? If that's not enough, there are multiple revenue streams for franchisees, expert support for franchisees, and a dedicated team, including a Travis Dickey descendant, to guide the brand at every touch point.

Southern cooking will never go out of style; neither will Dickey's style of franchising. Read the rest of the story, and then ask for more information.

—Dr. John P. Hayes

Dickey's Barbecue Pit:
Slow Smoked Nationwide

Slow-smoked, authentic, handcrafted and, yep, it's nationwide. There's just something about sharing a plate of ribs, creamy cole slaw, and "a cold one," that brings people together.

Barbecue smoked low and slow in a fast, casual atmosphere is an innovative concept that connects with guests' back-to-basics mindset. It's true. People may be busier these days, but they still want wholesome, quality comfort foods that they feel good about serving to their families— only a little quicker. Dickey's Barbecue Pit is taking barbecue mainstream, and doing something that no other brand has done before—bringing barbecue to a national audience, and eventually, an international audience. Who wouldn't want to be a part of that amazing opportunity?

There's Nothing More American than Barbecue

Dickey's Barbecue Pit is a true American success story. In 1941, Travis Dickey, a World War I veteran, opened the first Dickey's Barbecue Pit in Dallas, Texas. Dickey was an authentic Texas character, blessed with the gift of gab and the love of authentic, slow-smoked barbecue. Dickey's Barbecue Pit was a family operation, with Travis filling the smoker and working the block, and Miss Ollie Dickey serving sandwiches. Sons T.D. and Roland eventually took over the business in 1967, with big plans for expansion. Today, it's still a family operation.

Dickey's Barbecue Pit customers outside the original location in Dallas.

Dickey's Barbecue Pit became known throughout Texas for mouthwatering, hickory-smoked barbecue, popular catered events, and the iconic Big Yellow Cup. Travis Dickey's colorful personality, coupled with delicious pit-smoked meats, homestyle sides and tangy barbecue sauce, quickly made Dickey's Barbecue a household name. Franchising began in 1994 after loyal guests and barbecue fanatics demanded more locations. With 500 locations in 43 states by the end of 2014, and over 150 additional locations in development, barbecue has proven to be a smokin' hot business opportunity.

Barbecue is a smokin' hot business opportunity!

Is Your Mouth Watering Yet?

Today, Dickey's Barbecue Pit smokes all of its meats on-site in each restaurant the same way it was done in 1941.

The menu features beef brisket, pulled pork, and St. Louis-style ribs, along with an extensive array of homestyle sides from jalapeño beans to macaroni and cheese. Buttery rolls are served with every meal, along with complimentary ice cream. And just like always, kids eat free on Sunday.

At Dickey's Barbecue Pit, customers relate to the restaurant's hometown roots and authentic, down-home food, served with a signature brand of southern hospitality. But in today's fast-paced, quick-serve environment, creating a relevant brand takes strategy, innovation and sometimes a little hickory wood.

"We studied every concept out there, what they'd done right and where'd they'd gone wrong. I saw a lot of chains becoming what they're not. Others got confused about what their core values were," said Roland Dickey, Jr., president and CEO of Dickey's Barbecue Restaurants, Inc. in a 2014 interview in *Restaurant Business Magazine*. "Every company has to find a balance. You have to remain relevant to the consumer without surrendering your core values."

Roland is the grandson of the company's founder, and as a third generation trailblazer, he enthusiastically leads the charge today for global barbecue domination, one store at a time. Dickey's Barbecue is now officially the world's largest barbecue chain with no plans of stopping. Roland's passionate style has been a game changer in the fast casual restaurant industry and has made Dickey's Barbecue the fastest-growing restaurant brand in the country.

A Pretty Dang Classy Franchise

With the Dickey family still at the helm, Technomic named Dickey's Barbecue Pit the nation's fastest growing restaurant chain, and *QSR* Magazine named Dickey's Barbecue Pit the Best Franchise Deal. *Nation's Restaurant News* identified Dickey's as a Top Five Growth chain. The brand has come a long way from Travis Dickey's first location. As the fast, casual chain racks up recognition, the Dickey family still serves up the same quality barbecue recipes handed down from generations coupled with the same Southern hospitality, only on a much larger scale.

Dickey's knows it's the details that make customers come back, and attracts franchise owners to the barbecue business. The company offers one of the lowest start-up costs in the franchise industry, multiple revenue streams, and an expert support team for franchise owners. In addition, the construction and real estate departments assist franchise owners in site selection, lease negotiation, design, permitting and equipment procurement, while a dedicated marketing team guides the brand experience at every touch point. The company offers an extensive training program at Barbecue

University, where they drill down on their proven approach to quality, authentic barbecue and guest focus.

All Dickey's Barbecue Pit locations offer dine-in, to-go and catering options.

"I'm just as excited as the first day I stepped inside my new store," says multi-unit franchise owner Meg Heintzelman. "Five years after I made the decision to pursue Dickey's Barbecue, I couldn't be happier."

With almost 74 years under its belt, Dickey's Barbecue Pit continues to innovate and add to the guest experience. That's right, barbecue innovation. In 2011, Dickey's Barbecue Restaurants, Inc. beefed up catering sales by introducing a national catering hotline. Sales from the catering hotline channel have surged over the $5 million mark and continue to break monthly sales records, making Dickey's the No. 1 barbecue catering service in the nation. The national catering hotline vets almost 3,000 calls and online inquiries monthly, and this continues to be a key business channel for the brand. Now *that's* amazing!

"Catering sales continue to be a robust business channel for us," says Roland Dickey, Jr. "We're seeing continued expansion in this segment of our business—this includes both business-to-business and consumer catering."

Barbecue is not just for summer. In 2013, Dickey's Barbecue sold almost 20,000 holiday hams and turkeys. The holiday whole-meat options have become so popular that they've been added as permanent menu items. Dickey's also has a line of branded merchandise, including shirts, hats, rubs, sauces and *Mr. Dickey's Barbecue Cookbook* that offer franchise owners multiple revenue streams. And, who wouldn't love an "I Love Sauce" T-shirt?

Pit-Smoked Opportunity

Dickey's Barbecue believes in taking the same personal approach with potential franchise owners as it does with its pit-smoked meats. That is, it's important to get your hands dirty. For potential franchisees, this means getting to know their goals and lifestyles to make sure there is a good fit with a Dickey's Barbecue opportunity. Franchise owners don't need to have restaurant experience, but they do need to have a passion for barbecue. The development group really takes the time to explain the history of Dickey's Barbecue, franchise opportunities, and the company's expectations.

Dickey's Barbecue discounts franchise fees for all honorably discharged veterans who meet the franchise criteria. The barbecue brand was named a Military Friendly Franchise by *G.I. Jobs* and has multiple military veteran franchise owners who have been able to use their background and training to launch civilian careers with the nation's largest barbecue franchise.

"Our veterans provide a tremendous service to our country and Dickey's is honored to help make the dream of owning their own restaurant business a reality," explains Roland. "My grandfather, Travis Dickey, opened our first barbecue restaurant after his service in World War I and we continue our commitment to veterans today."

Classic with a Little Swagger...That's Dickey's

Today's consumer relates to brands that are authentic, straightforward, and genuine in their approach. Even though Dickey's Barbecue is recognized around the country, the company still wants guests to feel like they're in a local barbecue joint. From the rustic design of the restaurants, the wood fire smell from the smoker, to the tunes playing in the background—it all sets the tone for the customer experience. Dickey's Barbecue Pit doesn't take itself too seriously. But, they do take pride in the art of great barbecue and are fanatical about quality.

Dickey's Barbecue has become so much more than just a recognizable, national brand. They hold memories for many families. Guests spend their birthdays, graduations, weddings and important family events around Dickey's Barbecue, plus most have cabinets filled with Big Yellow Cups. Dickey's Barbecue Pit is a family concept with heritage that's been handed down from generation to generation, and a franchise system backed by a commitment to carry on the family tradition.

Like Mr. Dickey used to say, "If it's not messy, it's not barbecue." And at Dickey's, we speak barbecue!

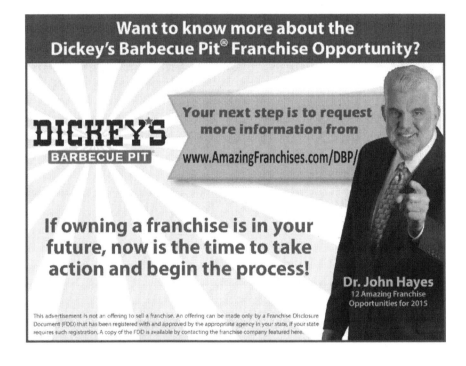

More than fast. More than signs.

You'll agree with me, I'm sure, that FASTSIGNS® is an amazing company for numerous accomplishments, but one in particular stands out: Military veterans get a 50 percent discount at FASTSIGNS, the largest discount afforded by any franchise company in the nation! Hooray for FASTSIGNS for giving America's veterans an opportunity to succeed as franchisees.

But what amazing quality attracts non-veterans as well as veterans to this seasoned company? How about the franchisee-financing programs? Start-up franchisees can apply for financing through Franchise America Finance, and FASTSIGNS also extends financing to franchisees through its own $6 million credit facility.

Of course, in the world of signage and visual graphics, FASTSIGNS continues to be a top-rated franchise opportunity year after year.

The company's average initial investment is as low as $178,207 for a franchisee with a net worth of $250,000. Franchisees consistently report that FASTSIGNS treats them well, beginning with its FASTSTART program that extends reduced royalties for a franchisee's first year so they have more money to invest in marketing their business.

This is a professional, highly-valued franchise opportunity that appeals to everyone who's thinking about building a business that serves the business community.

—Dr. John P. Hayes

FASTSIGNS: Turn Your Business Ownership Dreams into Reality

Turn your dreams of business ownership into reality as you embark on your journey to entrepreneurship. If you haven't researched the sign business before, you should consider the visual communications industry, which is a $29-plus billion annual industry. The world of signage and visual graphics is an exciting, rapidly expanding business, and FASTSIGNS continues to be positioned as the top-rated franchise opportunity.

What You Need to Know About FASTSIGNS

Founded in 1985 in Dallas, Texas, FASTSIGNS International, Inc. is the worldwide franchisor of more than 560 FASTSIGNS signs, graphics and visual communications centers in the U.S., Canada, the U.K., Brazil, Mexico, the Caribbean, Saudi Arabia and Australia (where centers operate as SIGNWAVE®).

FASTSIGNS provides comprehensive visual communications solutions to help companies of all sizes solve their business challenges. FASTSIGNS centers help businesses increase their business visibility with vehicle and floor graphics, point of purchase, labels and decals, architectural and interior décor signs, printing, promotional products and wearables, mobile marketing and other related marketing services.

As businesses look for new and better ways to compete with new media, FASTSIGNS capitalizes on this demand with products and services that extend well beyond traditional printing and include digital signage, QR codes and mobile websites.

Since 1985, FASTSIGNS has become a leader in one of the world's most dynamic franchise industries, with a growing network of over 560 locations worldwide.

The FASTSIGNS Opportunity

The average initial investment for a FASTSIGNS franchise is as low as $178,207 with net worth of $250,000 required. All of this information can be found in FASTSIGNS' Franchise Disclosure Document, which is required reading for any new franchisee. FASTSIGNS International provides candidates with the Financial Performance Representation document, which reveals unlimited earning potential. Financing is available with FASTSIGNS' $6 million credit facility and qualified candidates can put as little as 20 percent down.

New franchisees have access to financing through the Franchise America Finance program. FASTSIGNS is one of only a handful of franchises selected for this robust funding program, with $6 million in financing for approved franchise candidates. Plus, FASTSIGNS invests in franchise owners with the FASTSTART program that extends reduced royalties for your first year, so you can invest in marketing to build your business.

Discover Markets Available Worldwide

FASTSIGNS has approved over 400 markets for development in the U.S. and Canada. Through a targeted growth strategy, FASTSIGNS plans to open more than 50 locations each year for the next three to five years across the globe, entering 10 new markets. In addition to North American expansion, the company has specifically identified Central and South America, Quebec, India, the Middle East and Europe as international growth areas that have large business-to-business (B2B) sectors with a need for its services.

International Master Franchisees

FASTSIGNS is actively seeking master franchisees or area developers to expand into international markets. With these partnerships, the company's dominant brand name is shared with a proven business model in the visual communications industry and access to the latest technology, along with endless marketing resources and benefits.

FASTSIGNS recently signed master franchise agreements for growth in the United Arab Emirates (UAE) and North Africa. FASTSIGNS also recently expanded its Australian presence with a master franchise agreement.

The FASTSIGNS Ownership Benefits: Lifestyle and B2B Relationships

Owning your own business is one of the most important decisions you will make in your lifetime. FASTSIGNS provides the information you need to make a smart decision by helping you tie your business goals to your personal goals.

FASTSIGNS is a signage, graphics and visual communications partner that provides comprehensive solutions to help customers of all sizes—across all industries—meet their business objectives and increase their business visibility through the use of signs, graphics, printing, promotional products and related marketing services.

Franchising is a rewarding path to self-employment that provides you more control over your professional and personal life. As a FASTSIGNS franchisee, you can find the right balance between work and family. FASTSIGNS franchisees appreciate B2B working hours with no weekends or evenings.

FASTSIGNS allows you to control your future as you become involved in your community as a visual communications solutions provider for business customers from all industries. FASTSIGNS franchise owners enjoy a lifestyle of managing a low number of employees and building business-to-business relationships. Clientele are professional business people and owners. Other benefits are low staffing requirements and attractive margins.

Mark and Shawn Glenn, owners of
FASTSIGNS of Carrollton, Texas.

"FASTSIGNS continues to be the perfect business model for us to reach our personal financial goals," explains Mark and Shawn Glenn, owners of FASTSIGNS in Carrollton, Texas. "With the brand awareness, operational support, and the training resources, FASTSIGNS positions us to be the predominant visual communications leader in the market."

Veterans Take Advantage of Financial Incentives

FASTSIGNS offers military veterans the most comprehensive support and financial incentives available in the signage industry. FASTSIGNS participates in the International Franchise Association's (IFA) VetFran program that provides military veterans with special incentives and assistance to open a franchise. Veterans can take advantage of specific incentives, including a franchise fee of $18,750 (a savings of 50 percent) and reduced royalties for the first 12 months. FASTSIGNS is the only franchise in its industry to offer a 50 percent discount to any veteran, without stipulations. Now that's amazing!

Veterans Milton Guerrero and Woody Poole, both nuclear-trained Chief Petty Officers in the U.S. Navy, co-own their FASTSIGNS franchise in North Charleston, South Carolina. The partners met while serving.

"We began looking at franchises and FASTSIGNS instantly stood out from the rest," said Milton Guerrero. "We weren't just blown away by the business model—it was also the great resources and ongoing support they provide franchise partners."

If you're a veteran, ask for more information about FASTSIGNS' veterans program.

The Power of a Global Network

FASTSIGNS supports a mission of building sales and profitability for franchise owners. When you become a part of the FASTSIGNS franchise family, you enjoy the power of a worldwide network and name recognition that brings customers into the FASTSIGNS location.

You can minimize risk through FASTSIGNS' proven business method. New franchisees receive extensive training opportunities to learn about business operation and the visual communications industry. You spend four weeks in training with one week in a local FASTSIGNS center, two weeks at FASTSIGNS International's Dallas headquarters, and one week of onsite training in your new center. FASTSIGNS' franchisee mentorship program guides you with support in every aspect of your business.

Comprehensive Franchise Support

In an industry that's experiencing unprecedented growth, FASTSIGNS International, Inc. offers a leadership team that provides strong strategic direction. FASTSIGNS offers dedicated support in site selection and build out, training and mentorships.

Other benefits of the FASTSIGNS network include:

- ❖ Research and development of products and services.

- ❖ Ongoing business system and operational support.

- ❖ Network of peer owners.

- ❖ Buying power with FASTSIGNS National Accounts program.

- ❖ National Marketing Initiatives.

- ❖ National TV campaign.

The team at FASTSIGNS provides dedicated Business Consultants to assist you with business and financial training, marketing and sales, production and staff management. A team of Marketing Services Managers will help you with a pre-opening marketing blitz to drive sales and reduce ramp time. FASTSIGNS provides outside sales support to help train your sales staff and identify opportunities for new business.

Why You Should Choose a World-Class Franchise

As an industry leader for almost 30 years, FASTSIGNS has a proven track record of average gross sales and franchisee satisfaction. FASTSIGNS is a certified world-class franchise recognized by Franchise Research Institute. Other organizations have recognized FASTSIGNS for outstanding franchisee satisfaction and support, including Franchise Business Review and Canadian Franchise Association, with endorsements by franchise owners and scientific, confidential, third-party surveys. In addition to these honors, FASTSIGNS has been featured on the *Entrepreneur* Franchise 500 list for 15 consecutive years; ranked #1 sign franchise in 2011, 2012 and 2013.

FASTSIGNS has received both the Franchise Business Review FBR50 Franchisee Satisfaction Award Designation in the Business Services category and Canadian Franchise Association's Franchisee's Choice for over a decade and is recognized in the top 10 percent of the nation's franchises, receiving the G.I. Jobs Military Friendly Franchise award in 2012, 2013 and 2014. *USA Today* and *G.I. Jobs* magazine (2014) acknowledged FASTSIGNS for its commitment to the recruitment and advancement of veterans. *G.I. Jobs* magazine ranked FASTSIGNS in the top 10 percent of 4,000-plus franchise companies that are doing the most to recruit military veterans.

If you are looking for more out of life, the FASTSIGNS franchise opportunity is right for you. As a FASTSIGNS franchisee, you receive the power and training of a national brand, plus capabilities and support to help your new business succeed. The company's proven business model, high franchise partner satisfaction rankings, $6 million funding through Franchise America Finance, and a special incentive program for military veterans make FASTSIGNS the leading franchise opportunity in the sign and visual graphics industry.

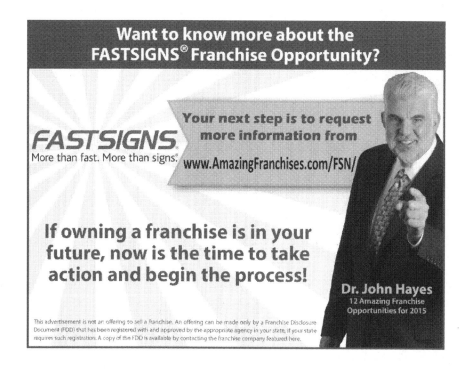

Franchising is a consolidating force that brings order and professionalism to every industry. For example, you're probably not old enough to remember when there were more independent pizza shops than franchised pizza shops, but take my word for it. Decades ago the pizza industry was not franchised, but once franchising caught hold, the franchised pizza shops dominated the industry. And they brought added benefits, such as consistent taste profiles, home delivery, and cheese in the crust!

So when you see franchising moving in to a disorganized industry, pay attention because monumental changes are about to occur and those changes create opportunities for entrepreneurs.

And that's why America's Swimming Pool Company is an amazing opportunity.

The franchisor of ASP recognized that independent pool service providers across the U.S. lack consistency and professionalism, and those are two hallmarks of amazing franchise opportunities. Those are also two qualities that consumers value, and once they find a company that delivers on its promises, consumers will remain loyal customers forever.

ASP is America's largest and most respected swimming pool maintenance, repair and renovation company. It provides franchisees with a home-based business and expert training. I'm enthusiastic about the company's leadership, and I expect we'll see more ASP franchisees throughout North America in the coming years.

—Dr. John P. Hayes

America's Swimming Pool: Uniting a Fragmented Industry

Search the Internet for a swimming pool company and nine out of the first 10 results are small, single owner/operator businesses. These results demonstrate the extent to which the swimming pool industry is fragmented—mom-and-pop companies are crowding local markets, leaving customers without a clear choice for their swimming pool needs. These local service providers tend to lack a consistent level of service and a unified professional image, leaving customers unhappy with the service they receive. This fragmentation has left the market ripe for a franchise system able to fill the void and provide a service nationwide that is absent in individual markets.

Stewart Vernon, founder and CEO of America's Swimming Pool Company (ASP) noticed this trend and opened a swimming pool service company in 2001 in Macon, Georgia. "I knew that any good service business solved a real-life problem for people. Realizing the issues in the pool industry, I set out to launch a business that would offer customers a level of service that just wasn't out there," explains Stewart. Through an apprenticeship with a local pool service expert who was preparing to retire, Stewart learned the industry inside and out. He invested a few thousand dollars to purchase service equipment and a truck, and began working as an owner/operator. By age 22, Stewart had successfully launched the first ASP location.

Over the next four years, business expanded so rapidly that Stewart opened a retail store, purchased more trucks, and hired employees to meet the growing demand for the high-quality standards now associated with ASP. Stewart was able to double his annual sales each year during those four years, yielding revenues of $1 million by 2005.

Dominating the Swimming Pool Industry

ASP—America's Swimming Pool Company—is the nation's largest and most respected swimming pool maintenance, repair, and renovation company. The mission of ASP is to provide high-quality swimming pool maintenance, service, and repairs at economical prices. The services offered by ASP include swimming pool maintenance, equipment installation, equipment repair, vinyl liner replacement, plaster repair, and swimming pool renovations. Providing these services feeds into ASP's ultimate goal of dominating the swimming pool industry.

Due to Stewart's motivation and the strength of his turnkey system, today there are 75 ASP franchise owners operating in 150 cities across 17 states. As a service-based business, most ASP owners run a home-based operation, reducing the overhead of maintaining office space and allowing them to quickly and easily scale the business to suit their markets and their needs.

From ASP's January 2014 annual Owner's Meeting. Owners gathered for two days of information, education and networking in Charleston, South Carolina.

Benefits of the ASP Franchise

Franchising ASP meant that Stewart would be able to expand his high-quality service expectations across the country, so that every pool owner could experience the same level of satisfaction and dependability. Additionally, the swimming pool industry is recession-resistant. Swimming pools are a large investment, and they need to be maintained and protected. There are about 11 million swimming pools in the American market, and nearly half of those pools are in the 10- to 15-year-old range. The numbers demonstrate that this market is poised for renovation work, which will contribute to the already growing $15 billion industry.

"A lot of people ask the question, 'Why a franchise?'" explains Daniel Fears, owner of the Covington, Louisiana franchise. "Anyone could go out there and open up a pool business, but ASP trains you on all the proper techniques, all the wiring, all the plumbing, how pumps work, and you can't get that experience and information opening up your own business. ASP has done more than just that. They train you from the basics of chemicals all the way to bookkeeping. Pool School has been phenomenal, and you couldn't ask for a better facility or group of people."

ASP's franchise system has been honed over years of success, and includes several specialized features. The resulting turnkey system provides business owners with:

❖ A proprietary, automated mobile platform that enables franchise owners to schedule, route, quote and report from anywhere in the field, making the most of precious time;

❖ An integrated communication system that sends automated emails to customers with testing results and technician activity, increasing customer satisfaction, loyalty and retention;

❖ A complete operations start up kit which includes the ASP Operations Manual, Quick Reference Guides, employee manuals, contracts, equipment repair books, and marketing operations data;

❖ A truck outfitting start up kit containing all of the required tools, equipment, materials and supplies to smoothly run a business using the ASP system; and

❖ ASP's intellectual property, including unique and profitable pricing models. These models implement annual service programs that provide a recurring revenue stream while offering customers simplicity and peace of mind.

"Stellar" Training & Support

With proven systems, training and support, new ASP franchise owners are set up for success. Pool School features on-site training pools and equipment for hands-on, innovative instruction in a realistic setting. Owners also service a local pool route, where there is ample opportunity to learn how to handle tasks that they will come across in the field. These tasks include installing and repairing equipment, balancing pool water, and even training on how to properly answer the phone. Pool School also teaches new franchise owners how to use the company's business software, and how to close sales.

ASP's two outdoor training pools allow new owners to gain experience treating, cleaning, and caring for two of the most common types of pool finishes—plaster and vinyl liners.

Franchise owner Clint Rowley in Phoenix, Arizona, says, "I have been part of the ASP family and system for just over two years and my experience has been nothing but stellar. I have a background in franchising and I can tell you that this organization has it together. Their systems are well thought out and detailed. The marketing is effective and easy to use and deploy. The accounting training was top notch and gives the owners all the tools they need to know exactly how healthy their business is, no matter their financial background.

Rowley continues, "The mentoring is detailed and supportive. The technical support crew is as knowledgeable as I have ever seen and has helped me not only diagnose problems, but quote jobs right in a client's backyard. The growth that we have seen here in Arizona has been amazing. We have beaten our goals that we set to achieve and the future is only brighter. We now have five full-time guys running routes and doing repairs. In one year, we have grown bigger than many of our competitors that have been in business for over 10 years."

ASP's indoor training facility allows new franchise owners to become familiar with the different types of equipment they will encounter out in the field.

After completing Pool School, franchise owners have access to a dedicated technical support staff that answers questions encountered in the field. Also, a business coach makes scheduled calls to franchise owners to ensure that everything is running smoothly, and to help solve problems that may arise. Additionally, ASP's operational support team makes field visits to every franchise location as many as three to four times a year to assess the owner's business, help identify problem areas, and provide solutions to ensure that each business is performing at the highest potential.

ASP's Lasting Value

Each franchise owner has the potential to generate unlimited revenues. "Every franchise owner is different, yet each has the potential to succeed and make the most of their business," says Stewart. Some are so successful that when the time comes, they can retire and sell their franchise.

Consider, for example, this letter from a former franchise owner upon the sale of his location:

Stewart and Tom,

Now that the dust is settling on the sale of my franchise, I want to take the time to thank both of you for the support you have given me over the years to make my investment with ASP a success.

A little more than five years ago I was surveying

franchises of all types, looking for the right business for my circumstances. I was at an age where I knew I had a limited time to work and I wanted a business I could develop into something I could sell to assist with my retirement.

During the first year, there were quite a few hot afternoons in customers' backyards on the phone with one or the other of you talking me through some task that had me stymied. There were a few times I thought I was going to have to leave the site with my tail between my legs and just acknowledge to the customer that I couldn't fix the problem. But you got me through it every time. I am appreciative of your patience.

Over the subsequent years the programs and support offered by ASP have enabled me to grow my business into a viable asset and the successful sale of the business has completed my five-year plan. As I retire, I want to acknowledge the role the two of you have played in my success and wish you the best with your plans to continue developing ASP as the premier pool service business in the country.

Sincerely,

Dan Meehan
Norcross, Georgia

Now that's an amazing testimonial that every franchisor hopes to receive from a franchisee.

Next time a pool needs cleaning, look up ASP. If there isn't a location in your area, consider opening one and bringing the quality and standards of ASP to a market that hasn't known the ASP experience.

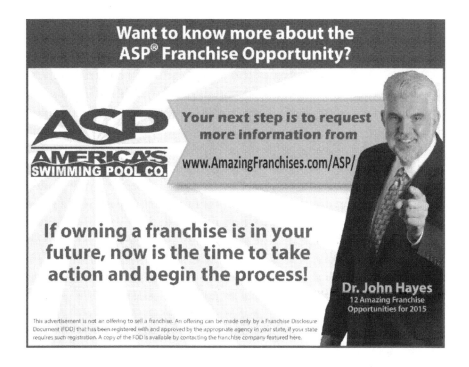

Imagine that a vicious hurricane displaces you from your hometown. You move to another city in another state where you meet up with another displaced victim. Instead of longing for what was, the two of you focus on the future. One conversation leads to another, and you decide to become business partners, open a "paint and sip" studio, and franchise it.

Sounds far-fetched?

Indeed, especially since neither partner had franchise experience, and some of their conversations occurred in a FEMA trailer in Louisiana!

But today it's another amazing franchise opportunity. Charles Willis and Craig Ceccanti created Pinot's Palette and began its development in the wake of Hurricane Katrina. It's a pretty good bet that had that hurricane never ripped through New Orleans, Pinot's Palette wouldn't exist today.

And it not only exists, but it leads the paint-and-sip franchise sector. By early 2014, there were at least 200 paint-and-sip outlets in North America, with new companies opening up almost daily. The concept creates a social experience where guests enjoy their favorite cocktails and snacks while learning to paint. Because it is a "no experience required" art event, the focus is on fun.

Of course, Pinot's Palette franchisees are also focused on making money, and co-founders Ceccanti and Willis created a technology suite that helps the franchisees operate their businesses professionally.

I think you'll want more information about this franchise opportunity!

—*Dr. John P. Hayes*

Pinot's Palette: Turning Disaster into a Business that's a Work of Art

In the fall of 2005, Charles Willis was living in a FEMA trailer and wondering what to do with the rest of his life. The destructive impact of Hurricane Katrina had left all of his possessions under eight feet of water and he was finishing graduate school at a remote campus while he looked for a new place to call home.

Displaced by the hurricane, Charles moved to Houston, and ultimately connected with a fellow Katrina victim, Craig Ceccanti. As they spent the next few months discussing their plans for the future, one idea kept coming up—a gallery-style setting in which groups or individuals could gather to socialize with a glass of wine while learning to paint.

Painting Class Leads to Business Idea

The seeds of the idea had been planted years before when Craig's mother had asked him and his brother to go with her to a painting class. The brothers said they would only go if they could bring some beer with them. It turned out to be a fun experience...and one that Craig would keep coming back to as an idea for a business.

They soon had their first location up and running in Houston, and just five years later, Pinot's Palette has become nationally recognized as the most innovative and creative franchise in the paint-and-sip franchise category.

Depending on preference and local requirements, partners may opt for a bar format or a BYOB format for their studio.

Where FUN and Business are a Perfect Match

Pinot's Palette puts a spin on the traditional girls' night out, date night, and corporate event by creating a social experience delivered in the form of a two- to three-hour painting event where guests enjoy their favorite cocktails and snacks. Because it is a "no experience required" art event, the focus is on fun and not precision.

Pinot's Palette provides the paintbrushes and easels, while a local artist guides visiting guests step-by-step through the process of recreating a featured painting. Although most Pinot's Palette locations are BYOB, many studios have built-in bars and also offer mobile studio options, depending on local laws or franchisee preferences.

Capitalizing on the recent trend toward customization, Pinot's Palette guests can tailor their experience to their own interests by choosing which specific painting they would like to recreate from an online portfolio.

Debra Nemec, who owns locations in Leawood and Prairie Village, Kansas, says that one thing she loves about owning a Pinot's Palette is that franchisees have as much fun as the customers.

"It's a business that markets fun," says Debra. "Owning a business like Pinot's Palette studios gives you the opportunity to work with people who are socializing and having a good time."

Pamela Bartlett, owner of the Naperville, Illinois location, was a stay-at-home mom who tentatively took the step into becoming a franchisee, not knowing what to expect.

"It's been a whole new chapter in my life," Pamela explains. "Pinot's is one of the best decisions I ever made. The business is unique, it is thriving, and I wouldn't want to be anywhere else."

Strong Presence in the Paint-and-Sip Sector

Through national partnerships with media, beverage companies, and retail chains, Pinot's Palette builds a strong presence and brand identity with its customer base. The corporate marketing team continually identifies national partnership and promotional opportunities that bring value not only to local partners in the system, but to the Pinot's Palette network as a whole.

As an entertainment business, Pinot's Palette constantly seeks to enhance the customer experience through added benefits. The national partnerships also allow Pinot's Palette partners to make the most of their marketing dollars by positioning themselves with a high-profile national chain.

Guerilla marketing is also an important part of the Pinot's Palette strategy.

"We are always looking for ways for our partners to maximize their profits," explains Craig Ceccanti, co-founder and CEO. "As part of the marketing support that Pinot's Palette provides, we assist our franchisees in developing marketing campaigns that engage their local communities and get them excited about our concept."

Pinot's Palette is an entertaining event perfect for Girls' Night Out, Date Night or private parties; the Pinot's Palette experience is about creating memories with friends.

Leading the Way in Technology

One big advantage that Pinot's Palette enjoys over competitors is a customized, proprietary technology system specifically designed to help franchisees save time, improve accuracy, and easily aggregate and analyze valuable data.

Whether franchisees are looking to discover more about their customers or looking for opportunities to increase sales, they have access to current data providing them with valuable insight into their business.

The technology systems are in place because Craig and Charles have strong backgrounds in technology and understood early on the impact a customized system could play in saving time and money.

"When we started out, we did payroll, seating charts, reservations, email reminders and other tasks manually," remembers Charles, co-founder and President. "I spent about 20 to 30 hours a week just doing administrative tasks needed to run the business. At the time we were on track to open two more studios. We realized that without a technology system designed for our specific needs, the business wasn't going to be sustainable."

Using the Pinot Technology Suite

Fortunately, it's always helpful to have an in-house computer programmer. Thanks to a background in computer science, Craig was able to create what is now known as the Pinot Technology Suite (PTS), a custom software platform catered to the paint and sip business.

"It's a lot like airline software," Craig reveals. "Each week we have hundreds of people who may attend a single studio. We have to account for changed reservations, folks who want to sit with their group of friends and also send event reminders to our customers."

In the end, PTS helps saves time, while also ensuring a seamless customer experience. But it doesn't stop there: The system also gathers valuable information to help franchisees strategize and stay ahead of the competition. "As a business owner, having detailed sales reports and being able to benchmark your performance is critical to growing a successful business," says Charles Willis. "PTS gives our partners the intelligence to know where their resources can have the most impact."

When it comes to marketing, calculating ROI accurately can be difficult if not nearly impossible. However, the PTS system enables franchisees to collect and store customer data. For example, an owner can easily run a report to see if the people who came by their booth at a festival also returned to their studio as a customer. By looking at this data, the owner has the power to determine if a marketing event was worth the investment.

A Network of Fun-Loving Franchisees

Dorothy Fadell, studio manager at the Staten Island, New York, location and owner of the Red Bank, New Jersey location, is a big fan of the Pinot's Palette technology, the executive team, and the ability of social media to bring franchisees together.

"They have the franchisee's best interests at heart, they're super responsive and they've created superior technology that tracks our business," Dorothy says. "And that's really important for a small business owner. They've created a Facebook page for franchise owners where we can go to meet other franchisees and share advice, ideas and our experiences."

Partners can customize their studios to reflect the local culture and community landmarks, making each location unique and one-of-a-kind.

Innovation is the Key

It may only have been in the last few years that paint-and-sip studios have cropped up across the nation, but the idea of enjoying art and wine as an entertaining pastime is nothing new.

Is painting and wine a concept that is here to stay? "We hear that question a lot," says Craig. "But truly, the key to building a long-term, successful business has little or nothing to do with the product or the service. Blockbuster was the dominant player in the movie rental space until a red vending machine put them out of business. The key to long-term success is innovation, and that is built into Pinot's Palette's value system."

That's what attracted Colleen Carlee, owner of the Montclair, New Jersey location. She knew immediately that Pinot's Palette was a perfect fit.

"We didn't have anything like Pinot's Palette in New Jersey," explains Colleen, who spent months researching potential franchises online before she discovered the paint-and-sip industry. "I was looking for something different and unique; I didn't want to do something that had been done before. And when I found Pinot's, I had a really good gut feeling."

That good feeling became even stronger after Carlee called Pinot's Palette headquarters and talked to Charles about franchise opportunities in Montclair. A few weeks after her initial phone call, she booked a flight to Houston to attend Discovery Day, the company's information session for potential franchisees. The trip gave Carlee an opportunity to get a feel for a typical studio's day-to-day operations, and, more importantly, it gave her a chance to attend her first-ever painting class.

"I loved it. I wanted to go back and take another class," says Carlee, who visited the company's original studio in Houston's Montrose neighborhood. "After that first class, I knew that this was a concept that would definitely work. I talked with the artist and the studio manager, and it just reinforced the feeling I had about the franchise."

With Pinot's Palette studios open across the country and more locations coming soon, the business has become the hot spot to share a drink and socialize. Pinot's Palette invites guests, who are innately curious and interested in deepening interpersonal relationships and celebrating creativity, to join in on their entertaining social event. Whether guests want to de-stress, connect with old friends or make new ones, or just tap into their creative powers, Pinot's Palette is the perfect night-out event...and a creative option for someone looking to get into business for themselves.

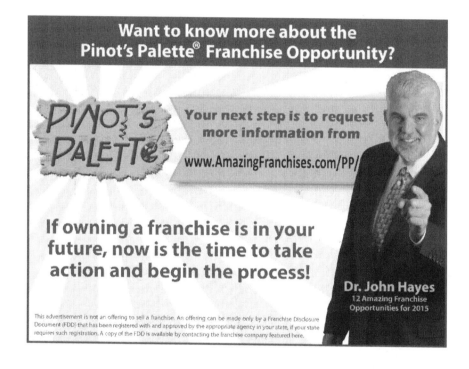

UNITED FRANCHISE GROUP

For years a franchise company was a franchise company, but nowadays many franchise companies own multiple franchise concepts. These franchise conglomerates, such as United Franchise Group (UFG), are amazing for many reasons:

- ❖ Depth of management and franchise experience;
- ❖ Cross-marketing opportunities to generate higher franchisee revenues;
- ❖ Buying power to lower costs for franchisees; and
- ❖ Multi-concept and multi-unit opportunities for franchisees.

United Franchise Group supports more than 1,400 locations in more than 62 countries—that's amazing, too—through five brands. We could have titled this eBook 16 Amazing Franchise Opportunities for 2015, but we've covered all five UFG brands in one chapter.

UFG's brands currently include SIGNARAMA, EmbroidMe, TransWorld Business Advisors, Plan Ahead Events, and Super Green Solutions. Each company has been designated as "best in their industry" by various franchise media.

With company-wide sales of $450 million annually, UFG's experience and vision for growth has led all of its brands to amazing levels of success. As a franchisee, you receive site selection and financing assistance, plus training and marketing tools to build your local business, generate new customers and increase repeat business.

If you're looking for a franchise opportunity that comes with a track record for success, and a highly skilled, passionate management team, ask for more information about UFG franchise opportunities.

—Dr. John P. Hayes

United Franchise Group: Helping Entrepreneurial Dreams Come True

It starts with a dream and a vision.

But making the dream of opening your own business and having entrepreneurial success come true takes more than just positive thoughts.

You need a system. Something that works. Something that has led to success time and time again.

United Franchise Group (UFG) knows what it takes. UFG helps business dreams come true. The company puts entrepreneurs into business with one of its award-winning franchise brands, but also knows that the franchisee must build the business right in their own community, helping other nearby business owners in the process.

With more than 1,400 locations in more than 62 countries, all of the UFG brands are focused on making a positive business impact in their hometowns. The tagline for the oldest brand, SIGNARAMA, recently changed to "The way to grow your business" to reflect its focus on advertising, marketing and branding solutions that can benefit local entrepreneurs. EmbroidMe is known as a "Promotional Marketing Partner" that helps its customers expand their business base. From event planning to energy solutions to business brokerage, UFG's brands help individuals attain their dreams of owning their own business. That's what propelled the company into a $450 million a year business with brands that are recognized for being the best in their categories.

UFG Global Headquarters in West Palm Beach, Florida

A Strong Foundation

The company's amazing story begins with United Franchise Group's CEO, Ray Titus. Having franchise pioneer Roy Titus as a father gave Ray unique insight into what it takes to grow successful brands. In the 8th grade, he wrote a school paper on how to start a franchise company. As an adult, he began working for his father, but by 1986 he was ready to go into business for himself, opening a small sign shop in Farmingdale, New York. Constantly innovating, he took that first store and eventually grew the brand into the world's largest sign franchise, now with nearly 900 locations in more than 50 countries. In the process, SIGNARAMA transformed what was once a handpainted craft into a high-tech and digitally focused industry.

"I credit my father, the late Roy Titus and founder of Minuteman Press International, for my foray into franchising. Through his influence, we grew from a single store into the United Franchise Group, a successful system of business-to-business (B2B) franchise brands and development services," says Ray.

Five Major Brands

Today the company includes industry giant SIGNARA-MA, the world's largest sign franchise; EmbroidMe, the world's largest embroidery franchise; SuperGreen Solutions, a one-stop retail location for energy efficient solutions; Transworld Business Advisors, a business opportunities brokerage franchise; and Plan Ahead Events, a full-service event management franchise.

UFG's experience and vision for growth has led all of its brands to tremendous success. The U.S. Department of Commerce, Franchise Direct and various other franchise and trade organizations have recognized UFG. *Entrepreneur* magazine has awarded all of the UFG franchise brands as leaders in their industries.

Former-President George W. Bush honors SIGNARAMA as the first franchise to receive the coveted Ecommerce Award

World-Class Support

The extraordinary success comes as the result of a solid foundation in franchising with a team that excels and has a passion for what they do. "Being a part of the UFG business model offers extensive benefits that simply can't be found anyplace else," explains Ray. It starts with a turnkey solution for those who want to build a solid business and future while maintaining a balanced quality of life. Achieving that balance is possible because of the system's established track record and proven procedures for operation.

As a franchisee, you receive assistance with site selection and the financing process to determine which of the UFG partnership lending programs is right for you.

If you want the best training, look no further than the opportunity provided by UFG. You'll travel to the global headquarters in West Palm Beach, Florida to attend a comprehensive, hands-on school, geared toward individuals with no prior experience or industry knowledge. This extensive education includes everything you need to know to run a business, and the industry knowledge you will need to succeed.

But it doesn't end there. Your education continues back in your location with on-site technical and marketing training to make sure you're ready to apply what was learned in the classroom to real-life situations right in your town.

"One of our local field representatives will provide one-on-one assistance on how to promote and develop your business. That same person, along with others, will always be able to support you with answers to any questions you may encounter as your business grows," continues Ray. UFG also provides ongoing educational opportunities for franchisees and their staff members through regional meetings and the World Expo. "Our proprietary online educational program ensures that you will always be able to benefit from industry updates and technological advancements without having to return for in-person training," explains Ray.

The Power of the Brands

The UFG brands are known throughout the world for providing outstanding products and services along with exemplary customer service. Living up to this reputation means building on a powerful brand awareness that every franchisee uses as a foundation for their business on a local level. Each franchisee learns the keys to success, which have been fine-tuned over 25 years, and each is given all the marketing tools they need to share those messages.

A full in-house marketing team is dedicated to providing all the print and digital materials needed to build each franchisee's local business, generate new customers and increase repeat business. The team works closely with advertising fund representatives to ensure the greatest synergies among marketing opportunities. The marketing experts are highly skilled in creating local marketing opportunities as well as online exposure to drive traffic to each location's website. Online marketing specialists work directly with the largest search engines to capitalize on UFG's strength in numbers so each franchisee gets the greatest online exposure possible.

Staying ahead of the technology curve is critically important in today's world, and no one does it better than UFG. Technological advancements extend beyond marketing and to various brand-specific applications including cloud-based point-of-sale systems for multiple brands and proprietary systems to manage and produce inventory. SIGNARAMA is the first sign franchise to offer online ordering, allowing customers to fully design and order signs from the website, anytime. The online technology team works with the research and development department to ensure that both are capitalizing on all advancements that could benefit franchisees.

UFG has an aggressive global growth strategy. Their brands can be found in countries around the world.

Maggie Harlow, who owns both a SIGNARAMA and Transworld franchise in Louisville Kentucky, puts it this way: "Being an entrepreneur demands that you never stop growing. You must keep up with the changes in the industry and technology. I look to role models for guidance, and United Franchise Group is full of them. It's the greatest benefit of being a part of this group—the wide range of people and experiences I can learn from to keep my business ahead of the never-ending learning curves."

Locally Owned, Internationally Grown

UFG brands are found in small towns and large metropolitan cities around the globe. That's because the systems are developed to work in different areas and are flexible enough to accommodate any differences in geography and culture. As pioneers in widespread global growth, United Franchise Group's Master License Program delivers a proven system with extensive training and support to help partners grow the brands successfully in their countries.

"The Master License Program enabled us to step into a franchise system that is well-developed with an unbelievable level of support. There's no need to reinvent the wheel, just follow a well-proven system," says Canadian Master Licensee Ghassan Barazi.

CEO Ray Titus made a commitment to growing UFG's brands internationally, and continues to lead the privately held company with a dedication to preserving the brands' reputations for innovation, exemplary support and high-quality products and services for business owners around the world. "As a franchisor, we are taking the role of leader and mentor, while promoting entrepreneurship worldwide. It's something I'm personally passionate about, and that we're passionate about as an organization," says Ray.

The passion of the organization shows in everything they do at UFG. From the massive annual World Expo events, to individual guidance and direction for each franchisee, there are an abundance of opportunities to learn, thrive and succeed. UFG is a family run business that's truly like a family, with a fundamental emphasis on growth and sales. Its core values emphasize a positive attitude and enthusiasm for the company, which is reflected in its mission statement: We have one customer: Our franchisees. When they are successful, we are successful.

If you are looking to own your own business, isn't UFG the kind of company you would want to grow with?

A ny franchise opportunity that comes with:

  ❖ Financial assistance for franchisees

  ❖ 9 to 5 working hours five days a week

  ❖ A van instead of an office

  ❖ No special education required

  ❖ And a guarantee...

can only be described as amazing!

And that's Dental Fix Rx, the only on-site dental equipment repair franchise in North America. I also like the fact that franchisees are up and running within 45 days, and 25 percent of the franchise network consists of veterans of the U.S. Armed Forces.

If you become a franchisee, follow the franchisor's systems for success but you do not sign 40 customers in your first year, Dental Fix Rx will refund your franchise fee. That's not just amazing, it's a sign of a confident franchisor.

With an aging North American population, there's a growing need for dentists and dental technicians, and they can't work without their equipment. Consequently, dental equipment repair is a $38 billion industry, and expanding.

This is a franchise opportunity that's smack dab in the midst of a booming industry, and that's one of the signposts for success for franchisees.

—Dr. John P. Hayes

Dental Fix Rx:
Like Weekends Off? We Have
the Perfect Franchise for You!

Having weekends off wasn't the reason why David Lopez created Dental Fix Rx in 2009. It was *a* reason, but not *the* reason!

The real reason, Scott Mortier, Vice President of Development, says, was to "offer smart, entrepreneurial-minded people with the opportunity to be the captain of their own ship, to have the ability to run a business, be an entrepreneur, but still have time for a family and a personal life."

What also makes Dental Fix different from many other franchise businesses is the fact that franchising was part of the equation from the start. It took only 90 days from the inception of the business before the first franchise was sold. And currently, Dental Fix Rx is the only on-site dental equipment repair franchise in the U.S. and Canada. Franchisees attend training at the headquarters, learn to repair and maintain dental equipment, train in a recreated dental office and work with existing franchisees on the job.

Most franchisees learn about Dental Fix from the news, through research or through friends. Known for its well-designed training program, almost anyone with even a remote interest in "fixing" things can run their own Dental Fix franchise.

"I was here for Discovery Day and went out in the field with my partner, and it helped a great deal," said franchisee Michael Leonard. "We learned a lot about how a dental office works and the technical aspects in everything from X-rays to sterilizers."

And, it's one of the few franchises offering a guarantee: If you purchase a franchise, follow the franchise model plan, and don't have 40 customers in one year, Dental Fix will refund your franchise fee. Now that's amazing!

With Dental Fix, the nationally-branded mobile van is the office.

With plans to expand, the franchise—just celebrating its 5th year anniversary this November—has already sold more than 150 franchises, and was named "Fastest Growing Service Franchise" by www.FranchiseOpportunities.com. The franchise has gone from a $1.5 million a year business by the end of 2010, to over a $16 million a year business by the end of 2013. Dental Fix is well on its way to exceed that figure by the end of 2014.

Why Dental Fix is Different

Other than the fact that franchisees can work the schedule of a dentist, often 9 to 5 during the week, a Dental Fix franchisee can have his/her business up and running in 45 days.

More differences? No building to lease or buy. No furniture or decorating. No heating and cooling bills from the local utility. With Dental Fix, the nationally-branded mobile van is the office.

After a six-week intensive training process including webinars, actual equipment repair and on-site dental repair instruction at Dental Fix's headquarters in Ft. Lauderdale, Florida, franchisees spend a week with trainers on-the-job in a regional van. The last week is spent with a new franchisee, learning and gaining invaluable experiences they can take with them when they start their own franchise. After gathering everything they need to know, franchisees have the support of a solid, well-oiled franchise system.

Even the Dental Fix van, which becomes each franchisee's "office," has been engineered for efficiency and functionality. Equipped with the latest and most reliable equipment and tools, franchisees perform their clients' repairs in their mobile office on-site, or as needed, in the doctor's office. The van is a comprehensive repair shop, containing all the essentials. There is no need for a brick-and-mortar office space.

The Dental Fix franchise model has thought of everything: From offering well-thought-out, strategic branding and marketing assistance, to contacting franchisee service-area dentists monthly, to advertising to local dental offices and generating online leads from the Dental Fix website and more. Dental Fix even assists with collecting past due invoices for franchisee services and repairs, freeing up time for franchise owners to focus on generating revenue.

Dental Fix Rx's top-notch training and franchise system was developed from the company's inception by serial franchisor and entrepreneur David Lopez, Dental Fix's CEO. David worked tirelessly with Mike Parker, a former dental entrepreneur, and Dental Fix's first franchise owner, to develop the Dental Fix business model. Armed with Mike's know-how and David's business acumen, an invincible franchise business model was born.

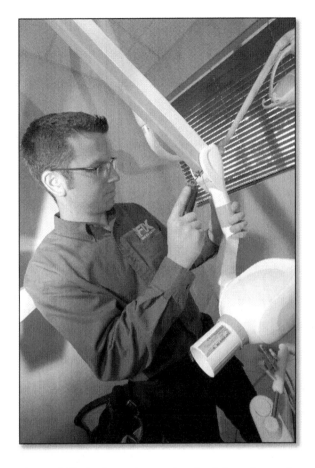

Dental Fix is the only on-site dental equipment
repair franchise in the U.S. and Canada.

Who is a Good Match for Dental Fix Rx?

Currently, 75 percent of Dental Fix franchisees are
owner/operators, meaning a franchisee works as a single
business owner with one van. This strategy works well for
those individuals who want to work for themselves and like

being their own boss, and want a Monday through Friday schedule. With this model, a franchisee's income depends on his or her desire to succeed. Dental Fix prides itself on hiring military veterans, and a full 25 percent of its franchise owners are veterans.

Another potential Dental Fix franchise candidate is an individual who would rather not manage other employees. Managing employees is a known stressor for business owners, and with Dental Fix franchisees this aspect of business ownership does not exist. The franchisee still has the opportunity every day to interact with dental office staff, but the responsibility and headache of employee management is left to the dentist, not the Dental Fix franchise owner.

You don't have to be mechanically-adept to learn dental equipment repair, either. "The training is very good and very in depth," explains new franchisee Ted Chen. "They started from the compressor room and then worked their way to the chair. I think they basically left no stone unturned as far as the training is concerned."

And for those who prefer a quiet, non-stressful work environment, what could be less stressful than working by yourself and for yourself? Each van is fully loaded with all the modern equipment needed, and if something cannot be repaired, Dental Fix franchisees can also sell new equipment and other dental office needs through the home office. Dental Fix has relationships with manufacturers, sellers, vendors and marketers to help franchisees generate revenue.

Franchisee Mike Loia inspecting
equipment on-site in a dental office.

But What Do Franchisees Have to Say?

"We get amazing feedback all the time," says David Lopez, Dental Fix's CEO. "We regularly send a survey to our franchise owners asking them if they would refer the franchise to a family member or friend. This is one of the metrics used to determine the bonus for the management team in the company. Our franchisee satisfaction has improved every quarter for the last four quarters straight," he adds.

Brad Cox, a new Dental Fix franchisee, had been working for 15 years in a corporate environment when he "realized the corporate lifestyle wasn't really what I wanted to do....I researched different companies where I could be my own boss, and found Dental Fix...where I could control my own future," Brad explains. "Discovery Day was great. You know, when you decide you're going to look at this franchise, you don't know anything about dental. But once you come and see it, you realize, 'Hey, I can do this.'"

"When you come to the corporate office you ride around with a technician already out in the field who is doing (the business)," adds Brad. "You can see what goes on in the doctors' offices ... and how the process goes and you realize it's not rocket science and you can get it done through training. It's incredible."

Franchise owner Michael Leonard of San Antonio, Texas, agrees. "Dental Fix has given me the freedom as a business owner to make great money and have nights and weekends off, too," he says.

Dentists have found that Dental Fix meets their needs as well.

Dr. Ken Tralongo, of Atlanta, Georgia, is pretty clear about his preferences, saying, "Forget who you used in the past. Dental Fix is the best option for service and equipment."

How Much Does it Take?

With a 45-day start-to-finish training and franchise start-up timeline, Dental Fix franchises provide one of the fastest ways to get a new franchise business off the ground and up and running. Franchisees don't have to have any background in repair or dental services to be successful.

Dental Fix also offers help with financing for franchisees at attractive rates.

Dental Fix's Scott Mortier estimates a franchisee can charge approximately $150 to $200 per hour and can see up to five dental offices a day. Franchisees get a protected territory and a personal account manager at the home office to help each franchisee start out successfully and remain successful.

"Typically, the costs range from $125,000 to $160,000 for the ownership fees, six weeks of training, inventory, equipment, repair tools and the van," says Scott. "With the financing we have available most owners only need about $25,000 in cash and we can get them financing for the rest of the money needed."

What's in It for Franchisees?

Fixing dental equipment is a $38 billion industry. Yes, billion!

There are approximately 190,000 dentist and dental specialist jobs in the U.S., and dental industry positions are projected to grow nine percent through 2016. Dental equipment is expensive and as it ages repairs are necessary to keep the practice open. With dentists becoming even more necessary as the U.S. population ages, there will be a greater need for additional dental pros such as dental implant specialists, orthodontists and other dental professionals.

As more specialists come on board, the need for repairs and service will have a positive financial impact on Dental Fix franchisees. Even new equipment needs servicing, sometimes costing a dental business a lot of money if equipment is down, meaning a mobile, on-site repair service will become even more attractive to dental offices across the board. And with a lagging economy, dental practices are holding onto their existing equipment longer. Old equipment needs fixing, and with a reliable, on-site service professional just a call away, many dentists see the benefit of repairs on-site rather than waiting for parts from other service providers.

Where is Dental Fix Headed?

According to Dental Fix's CEO, David Lopez, the sky is the limit. "The potential for Dental Fix is endless as it is the only on-site dental equipment service franchise in the industry," he says. "It's been another tremendous year for us as we build on our brand's success and continue to grow throughout the United States and Canada."

And potentially other international markets. But for now, the U.S. and Canada have tremendous opportunities for the franchise. In addition, Dental Fix sees tattoo shops and veterinary offices as potential clients for franchisees. Once established, franchisees can serve these other businesses as well, increasing the client base beyond dental offices.

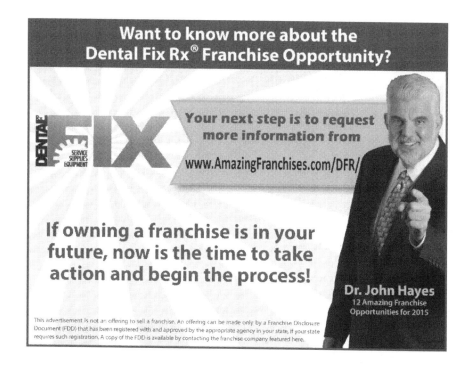

There are many accolades that I can use to describe Jani-King, a company that I've known for some 25 years. But what's most amazing about Jani-King is that it offers a franchise opportunity that appeals to people regardless of their socioeconomic class, education and financial status.

While Jani-King attracts franchisee investors who have accumulated years of business experience (and the money to show it) the company also attracts franchisee investors who are just getting started in business. In fact, some are starting out part-time. Some franchisees build large, multi-city or regional operations, while other franchisees are content to confine their business to a smaller area. Again, it's a franchise opportunity that meets the immediate needs of franchisees, but provides ongoing growth opportunities.

From its inception, Jani-King has been an amazing company. Imagine sleeping in your car for months just to get a new business off the ground. That's what Jim Cavanaugh did to establish this franchise. And it wasn't an exotic business; it was cleaning! Many thought he was wasting his time and talent, but he believed otherwise because he realized the potential of franchising. As a result, Cavanaugh built what has become the "king" of cleaning with franchisees across North America and in numerous countries.

When it comes to the cleaning industry, Jani-King is one amazing opportunity.

—Dr. John P. Hayes

People, Pride and Performance Abound at Jani-King

Scrubbing counters and buffing floors may not immediately come to mind when researching franchise opportunities, but this company is going to change that.

Consider this: Jani-King franchisees manage cleaning services at hotels, hospitals, schools, offices, retail centers, manufacturing facilities, restaurants and event facilities, including the world's largest stadiums. Now, if you realize those facilities need to be cleaned every day, every week, every month, and every year, you quickly appreciate the amount of recurring revenue that is generated in this amazing industry.

According to the U.S. Bureau of Labor and Statistics, the commercial cleaning industry is a $100-billion service machine that is projected for even more growth.

Jani-King's founder recognized this opportunity decades ago. In fact, he founded Jani-King in 1969, and five years later, Jim Cavanaugh was the first to transform his commercial cleaning company into a franchise powerhouse, one that would lead the charge in raising the service bar of an entire industry.

Taking Care of Business

Jani-King's franchise model was built on the concept of People, Pride and Performance. And today, the company continues to thrive on that same concept; people who have pride in the business they own and operate will perform to greater standards. Look at it this way: When you rent a car, do you take care of it with the same passion as you do the car you own? No, because it's not yours. The same concept applies to owning your own commercial cleaning business. You've made an investment of several thousand dollars, so now it's time to take care of that investment. Jani-King franchisees take care of their investment by taking care of their customers' the cleaning needs. Without satisfied customers, franchisees can't grow their business. And without that pride of ownership, customers are just getting another conventional service provider whose concept does not include owner/operator franchisees.

This concept, along with the right training and support, delivers results to customers more consistently and to higher standards than the traditional employee/supervisor role.

As mentioned, Jani-King was among the very first franchised commercial cleaning companies, and being the world's largest has its advantages. First, you are a leader in bringing your concept to market, giving you a leap on any future competition. Secondly, you have an opportunity to learn from your franchisees and develop systems early on that help support and promote their business. Being the largest also gives you the experience, results and passion to continue to strive to be the best. There is no rest for the industry leader. There is only more work that needs to be done in order to stay ahead of the competition and retain the title as The King of Clean.

Jani-King has specific training programs for
specialized accounts including hotels and resorts.

For more than 40 years, Jani-King has done just that. The company stands today as the world's largest commercial cleaning franchisor with operations and regional support offices in 14 countries. In the U.S., there are 87 regional support offices. Through the company's global headquarters and support offices, franchisees receive training, administrative assistance, operational support and access to equipment, marketing materials and technology that improves the performance of their business.

Helping Franchisees Feel Comfortable

For many entrepreneurs, starting out in their own business can be a challenging and even scary experience.

- ❖ Are you hesitant, or even afraid, about approaching potential customers and initiating a conversation or making a sales pitch?
- ❖ Do you have enough money for equipment or an office space to lease?
- ❖ Do you have the software to invoice customers and the ability to collect on monies due?
- ❖ How are you going to find new customers, execute a proper bid for services and sign a long-term contract?

While these are all necessities of starting a new business, they can be intimidating for new entrepreneurs. This is where Jani-King's franchise model comes in and helps franchisees get started in their new business.

From lobby areas to restrooms to floor care,
Jani-King franchisees provide professional
cleaning services you can count on.

Jani-King regional support offices are staffed with sales professionals who spend their day prospecting for new customers and signing new accounts to offer to franchisees.

Even the investment in a Jani-King franchise comes with a guarantee of initial business offerings, based on which franchise plan you choose. As you continue your Jani-King franchise, you can accept additional accounts to service from Jani-King, or you can solicit new accounts on your own by using Jani-King's marketing materials.

Another major obstacle that is avoided when you invest in a Jani-King franchise is the need to purchase or lease an office space. All franchisees have access to their local Jani-King regional office, or you can work out of your home. Equipment can be kept at your house or, in many cases, left at the customer facility in a janitor's closet. The regional office is there to provide account billing, collections, training, and overall support of your Jani-King franchise. This leaves you with time to focus on hiring and managing employees to clean facilities and build relationships with customers.

Customer Referrals Add Revenues

Jani-King has a strong portfolio of successful franchisees that understand the importance of customer service. Many franchisees grow their business by building relationships with customers and getting referrals for new business. These customer referrals mean two things:

1. That the customer is satisfied and you are likely to keep that account year after year, and

2. The customer is willing to help you grow your
   business by referring you to new opportunities.

Referrals aren't the only way to grow your commercial cleaning business. Jani-King implements national marketing strategies that promote the their brand to facility managers and commercial property owners throughout the industry. For example, Jani-King is a national partner with the Professional Golfer's Association (PGA) of America as well as the Bowling Proprietor's Association of America (BPAA). Those partnerships help deliver opportunities to potentially clean thousands of golf course country clubs and bowling centers across the nation. Jani-King also has partnerships with professional sports teams, colleges and universities, cleaning equipment manufacturers and other industry-related organizations. All of these partnerships create exciting marketing platforms for Jani-King to drive new business to franchisees.

Partnering with industry organizations also develops industry experts within the Jani-King system. Jani-King's specialty divisions are staffed with experts in their respective fields. The representatives in those departments are trained in that specific field or industry, have years of prior experience working in those facilities (such as hotels, hospitals and stadiums), and continue to further their knowledge. That information is then delivered to franchisees through training and other learning opportunities at the regional office level.

Again, all of this experience and effort helps franchisees grow their business.

Turnkey Solution

In an industry such as commercial cleaning, one where new buildings are constantly being erected or old buildings renovated, it is easy to see why there is projected growth. Additionally, state and federal guidelines regarding cleaning standards in hospitals continue to evolve and create new opportunities. Demands of guests and easy access to online reviews make it critical for hotels to retain top-notch house-keeping staff. Schools are leaning on custodians to help keep kids in school by reducing germs and providing a healthy environment. Sports teams are building bigger and better stadiums and therefore require bigger and better cleaning services.

Major corporations and small businesses alike are all watching their bottom lines and turning toward outsourcing their commercial cleaning as a way to save money. Out-sourced janitorial services can create significant cost savings when you figure in the costs of employee hourly rates, over-time, insurance and time that management spends hiring and training cleaning staff. Jani-King offers those companies a turnkey solution by taking over cleaning duties and creating a value solution for management.

By eliminating germs on high-touch surfaces, Jani-King franchisees are helping to keep customers and employees healthy in the workplace.

Imagine Your Future with Jani-King

Still not convinced that a future with vacuums and trashcans is right for you? Imagine what that future can actually look like when you manage your franchise effectively.

❖ You're based from your home, building relationships with customers and ensuring that your employees are well-trained and performing the proper services.

❖ You're generating recurring revenue. This is

important because as each day passes, you have an opportunity to increase your revenue month after month with each new account that is signed. You're a small business in your local community and you're supported by a local, regional office.

❖ You're a part of a global franchise system that has buying power, brand recognition and is well-respected around the world. You're also respected by other local businesses as a key service provider in their formula for success.

Remember, this isn't a rental car. This is your opportunity to own a business that you can be proud of, and one that can help you reach your goals while helping your employees and customers be successful. At Jani-King, it's been said that there's money in dirt. It's time that you gave the commercial cleaning industry a real look.

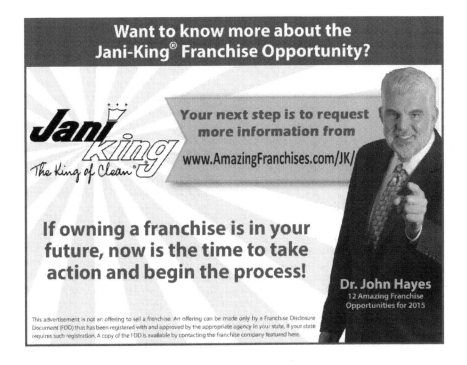

What smokers want most is to quit smoking, and now, amazingly, comes Palm Beach Vapors to help smokers do exactly what they want. According to the Centers for Disease Control and Prevention, 69 percent of smokers want to quit, and many of them are looking for alternatives. Thus, they've created the new and expanding "vaping" industry.

Smokers hope to quit their habit for obvious health reasons and cost savings, which not only include the rising cost of cigarettes, but exorbitant dry cleaning bills to keep their clothes from stinking. Tobacco has been the major cause of preventable disease globally for many decades, so this is one nasty habit to give up!

Palm Beach Vapors is America's premiere franchise opportunity retail vapor store with an impressive business model that requires less than $100,000 for start-up. Smokers who've decided to quit visit Palm Beach Vapors for vapor juice, filters, equipment, and sometimes, moral support.

Each store includes a trademark Tiki Hut for sampling a variety of juices.

Franchisees make their own juices, which is not only best for quality control but also for profitability. The franchise opportunity has been designed to help franchisee seekers get into the vaping business quickly and successfully.

—Dr. John P. Hayes

Palm Beach Vapors: Capitalize on Helping People Quit Smoking

Although the last several decades have shown a steady decline in tobacco smoking, it remains a top health risk and killer. In fact, over 440,000 people died last year from cigarette-related illnesses, and any business that helps people break the habit of smoking seems to be a great business. Palm Beach Vapors is the premiere franchise opportunity retail vapor store with a business model that is truly impressive. They are educating and inspiring customers to use "vaping" as a means to reduce their health risk caused by smoking, and finally quit.

Two of the amazing aspects of this franchise, in addition to helping people improve their health and live longer, include:

❖ Customers visit Palm Beach Vapors regularly for vapor juice, filters and equipment updates.

❖ Palm Beach Vapors franchisees make their own juice, which is not only best for quality control, but also for profitability.

Helping People Stop Smoking—
Incredible Growth Opportunity

Today, about 20 percent of the U.S. population is comprised of smokers, and 50 percent of people have smoked in their lifetime. Smoking has become less socially acceptable, and people are not ignorant to the health risks. "Vaping" offers a great solution. It has proven to be one of the best ways to quit smoking, enabling smokers to slowly dial down their nicotine while they enjoy the almost unlimited flavors available in "vaping" juice. Smokers now have a cool apparatus that emulates smoking, and they get to try all kinds of flavors. People of all ages, backgrounds and income levels are becoming vapor users.

Brand Leader in Vapor Industry

Palm Beach Vapors is among the first to launch a franchise opportunity, and has come out of the gate extremely strong with 12 operating units in just two years. Until now, "vaping" supplies could be found at convenience stores, head shops and a growing number of independent operators. Palm Beach Vapors' retail stores offer customers a comfortable and secure place to shop, try different juice flavors and learn about new trends. New customers are offered the opportunity to "take the pledge" and make a choice to stop smoking right then and there. How amazing is that?

Convenient locations for frequent visits by
customers who want to stop smoking.

Turnkey Business—Low Investment

If you have ever launched a new business it is never as easy as it seems. Your mistakes end up costing much more than you planned. That's another reason why franchising with Palm Beach Vapors makes sense.

The Palm Beach Vapors franchise opportunity has taken the guesswork, research time, and unnecessary expense out of launching a vapor store. The turnkey franchise opportunity provides everything you'll need to start your business, including their proprietary trade secrets, operating systems and support for the life of your business. The investment covers all of the interior décor, cabinets, start-up inventory, vapor juice and much more. Franchisees need to have adequate working capital and marketing dollars, as is true of any business, but you can launch a Palm Beach Vapors retail store for under $100,000.

Customer Loyalty and Frequency

When it comes to retail businesses, building loyalty and frequency is the key to growing revenues. Palm Beach Vapors stores are all about creating the best customer experience possible, and they use education and strong customer service skills to build trust and loyalty. And with the word out about "vaping," more and more people are looking for Palm Beach Vapor stores to see what it takes to stop smoking. Customers come to Palm Beach Vapors for education almost as much as for buying products. A trained staff offers customers professional assistance and advice, and treats customers with compassion.

Customers are made comfortable and encouraged to ask questions. Once a customer purchases their "vaping" gear from Palm Beach Vapors, they typically become a regular customer for a monthly supply of vapor juice and filters. When they are ready for a stronger battery, or the latest equipment, they return to Palm Beach Vapors. The stores gain referrals from successful and happy customers who are weaning themselves off tobacco in an enjoyable and relatively easy way.

Is Palm Beach Vapors a Good Fit for You?

Another amazing point about Palm Beach Vapors is that people from all different careers and backgrounds can do well with the business. If you had retail or management experience it would be a plus, however, you mostly need to be a self-motivated, intelligent person with a desire to reach financial independence. Palm Beach Vapors franchisees all seem to share one thing in common: They care about people and take great pride in helping people quit smoking. They are saving lives by helping people in their community finally quit.

Palm Beach Vapors doesn't require franchisees to be full-time owners/operators. In some cases, managers operate the stores on behalf of franchisees. Palm Beach Vapors stores also make great family businesses, allowing the convenience and flexibility that most families appreciate.

Launch Your Store Within 90 to 120 Days!

Palm Beach Vapors has made opening and operating a store as easy as possible with streamlined operations to include purchasing, inventory control, staffing and daily sales activities. Their point-of-sale system also makes it easy for franchisees to manage sale transactions and initiate reporting.

Palm Beach Vapors' criterion for site selection takes into consideration market demographics, competition, traffic, access to location, parking, neighboring businesses, market outlooks, and more. Selecting the right site is essential to the success and longevity of your business.

Store interiors include a Tiki Hut for tasting different juices.

The franchisor also has simplified interior store requirements to make the "build-out" into a simple remodel of an existing location. The "Make Ready Package" includes everything a franchisee needs to open a store. Furniture, fixtures, decorator items, neon sign, and wall graphics are included. Opening inventory is included in the package, as is a Tiki Hut for the store vapor bar. The island theme brings together bright colors and wood tones that provide Palm Beach Vapors' customers with an incredible brand experience.

Compared to other retail businesses, the inventory investment for a Palm Beach Vapors location is modest. The initial package includes a starting inventory of products and vapor juice. The franchisor teaches franchisees how to work with suppliers and to know the most popular products. Palm Beach Vapors provides professional training on all aspects of the business. Their comprehensive operations manual provides detailed information and instruction about how to operate every aspect of a Palm Beach Vapors store.

One of the biggest advantages of joining Palm Beach Vapors is their commitment to franchisee success. The company is focused on continual improvement of average unit revenues and year-to-year same-store sales growth. The franchisor's support team is only a phone call away and is prepared to share best practices and business metrics. Independent operators do not have the luxury of a support team or knowledge about best practices and metrics, and they often fail for these reasons.

Brand Marketing and Public Relations

Franchise history has demonstrated that being first to market offers some great advantages. Palm Beach Vapors is not the first vapor business, but it is first in creating a retail vapor store franchise system and rolling out a "national brand." As the company continues to grow, their brand equity will not only become a valued driver of new business, but will translate into equity in the business. The Palm Beach Vapors brand identity is unique and loved by customers for its no-pressure, comfortable environment.

"Vaping" offers a great solution for those who want to quit smoking.

Palm Beach Vapors is a tech-savvy franchisor and has deployed resources to develop and manage a new website. Each franchisee can gain exposure online with a local microsite, making it easy for customers to find them online. In addition to online marketing and search-engine optimization (SEO) practices, Palm Beach Vapors stores do quite well with grassroots marketing. The Palm Beach Vapors team shares best practices and provides a host of marketing templates to streamline marketing implementation.

Palm Beach Vapors also utilizes public relations to gain local news coverage and promote store services. Local and national media are interested in the vapor/e-cigarette business, so they will frequently promote grand openings and special events at the stores.

Why Choose Palm Beach Vapors?

If you gravitate to a business that has a growing demand, strong unit economics, and offers a worthwhile product or service, Palm Beach Vapors offers a great value to someone looking to get into business quickly without leaving anything to chance. CEO Chip Palm is an experienced businessman with a background in franchising. His passion for the business has fueled its growth and positioned the business as a leader in the retail vapor market.

POSTNET

Do you see yourself as a consultant to entrepreneurs and local businesses? If so, PostNet may be the best franchise opportunity for you. PostNet franchisees focus on helping small businesses succeed by providing a wide range of products and services, all from one convenient location.

PostNet franchise owners offer a full range of print services, website design, email marketing, direct mail, consultative marketing support, and shipping and logistics solutions. These services make it easier for business owners to create professional marketing materials, which in turn help them reach prospective customers.

PostNet serves as an outsourced marketing and logistics partner for small businesses and takes away the challenge of small-business owners having to do this work themselves. Instead, they can let PostNet go to work for them, while they concentrate on running their businesses.

By providing value-added, consultative support, PostNet has been able to grow to hundreds of locations throughout the United States, and hundreds more worldwide. Franchisees learn a comprehensive, three-step program that teaches them how to cater to small businesses.

For years I've watched the PostNet corporate team develop their franchise network. What I value about them is their honesty, passion, and their commitment to doing everything that's possible to help their franchisees succeed. This is one amazing success story!

—Dr. John P. Hayes

PostNet: The Business that Helps Small Businesses Succeed

Are you interested in joining a franchise that can make a big difference in your community? How about starting a business that is uniquely positioned to help others succeed? That's the heroic niche served by PostNet, which provides printing and marketing solutions that help other businesses grow.

Small businesses power the American economy. In fact, they're responsible for two-thirds of the net new jobs created since the 1970s—and PostNet powers small businesses by making it easier for them to get and keep more customers.

With the help of the Denver-based franchise, PostNet owners offer a full range of print services, website design, email marketing, direct mail, consultative marketing support, and shipping and logistics solutions. Together, these services make it easier for business owners to create professional-looking marketing materials and then effectively distribute them to reach prospective customers.

Help Build a Stronger Country

"If our country is going to stay strong, we've got to focus on small businesses and help them succeed, and it's exciting to know that we are part of that," says Irene Fenolio, who owns a PostNet in Henderson, Nevada, with her husband, Ron.

PostNet's wide range of services and products also makes it easier for small-business owners to get everything they need at one convenient place.

The marketplace for these services is huge: Digital printing, online marketing and shipping generate more than $380 billion in revenue each year, but it can be difficult for America's 27 million small businesses to access and use these services. PostNet serves as their outsourced marketing and logistics partner, taking the challenge out of doing it for themselves. By providing value-added, consultative support to entrepreneurs and businesses, PostNet has been able to grow to hundreds of locations throughout the United States, and hundreds more worldwide.

The "Make It Go Away Place" for Busy Entrepreneurs

Small-business owners juggle a lot of responsibilities and often work long hours.

Kathy and Rick DeMatteo with a customer
at their downtown Denver PostNet.

Terry Stokes, who owns a PostNet in Steamboat Springs, Colorado, with his wife, Kathy, describes the customer relationship this way: "We are the 'make it go away place.' Customers trust their printing, shipping or marketing projects with us, often with urgent deadlines, and just want to know we can get them done professionally and on time. That's where we shine."

The fact that PostNet centers are locally owned and operated also appeals to entrepreneurs who enjoy working with fellow small-business owners they can turn to when they need help.

Nathan Moore owns a business in Asheville, North Carolina, that helps restaurants manage their equipment, and he goes to PostNet for creative services like graphic design, booklets, trade-show displays and more. He says

Asheville PostNet owner, Bill Merwitzer, has become a trusted friend. "I would never call them vendors; they are business partners," Moore says. "They really care about their customers' success."

Customer loyalty and comprehensive services lead to long-term business relationships and a lot of repeat business for PostNet owners.

How PostNet Owners Do It!

PostNet owners enjoy tremendous support from the company, which has designed a business model that empowers local franchise owners to offer its wide range of services and products without having to be an expert at everything.

PostNet's comprehensive three-step training program teaches new franchise owners how to consult with business owners to identify exactly what they want and need. Once the needs have been determined, PostNet franchise owners use a proprietary technology platform to generate a professional quote for the project. The technology platform enables owners to quickly determine whether they can best meet their customers' needs by working with an outsourced partner or by providing in-house production. These partnerships allow PostNet franchisees to handle many types of jobs without having to own costly, specialized equipment, and to enjoy great profit margins—often in excess of 70 percent—for acting as a project manager on behalf of clients.

"Building profitable partnerships is just one of the ways we help our franchise owners increase revenue and improve profitability," says Brian Spindel, PostNet's President and COO.

PostNet's graphic design, printing and logistics services allow franchisees to provide back office support to small business owners.

Top Five Reasons Franchisees Love Being Part of PostNet

PostNet franchisees enjoy owning their Neighborhood Business Centers for a lot of reasons, but five things stand out:

- ❖ **The business has unlimited potential.** While PostNet owners enjoy a protected territory, there are no restrictions on where franchisees can market or sell their products and services. Many PostNet owners do business with organizations, institutions or companies with multiple offices, and there is never a shortage of customers that want, need and use PostNet's products and services.

- ❖ **You can have a life and build something for your family!** Unlike most food or retail businesses, PostNet Neighborhood Business Centers have sane hours of operation—typically 9 a.m. to 6 p.m., Monday through Friday and a half day on Saturday. That means you can be home evenings and weekends instead of powering through the 16th hour of an endless workday. Many PostNet businesses are also family businesses. Husband-wife, mother-daughter and father-son teams are common.

- ❖ **It's not a fad, flavor or trend.** People and companies will always need to send and receive things, create high-quality materials, and operate and compete effectively in the digital world. By being committed to evolving with technology and consumer needs, PostNet will always be at the forefront of what customers want and need!

❖ **They make a positive impact.** Because PostNet Neighborhood Business Centers are knitted into the fabric of their communities, they add value and help improve and enhance the businesses and lives they touch. PostNet is a business where you can and do make a positive impact in the community.

❖ **The relationships within PostNet.** PostNet's culture, technology and communications platform enable and encourage franchisees to share ideas, build relationships and help each other. This is probably one of the most unique and amazing aspects of being a PostNet franchisee.

Culture and Values

For such a large franchise system, the franchisees at PostNet are extremely tight-knit. PostNet's CEO and co-founder, Steve Greenbaum, believes that the company's vision, culture and values establish the foundation on which those relationships are built. "We attract people who share our passion for business and for people. PostNet is an organization that truly cares about everything and everyone the brand touches."

PostNet encourages an open and inclusive culture among its franchisees. PostNet also supports a National Franchisees Advisory Council that helps review new services and products and technology initiatives, and that serves as the voice of the franchisee within the organization. The company has an active internal communications system that makes it easy for franchisees to share advice, ask questions and get quick answers if they encounter a unique situation.

"The collaborative, congenial atmosphere has been a great, wonderful surprise and is a reason we're still here with no desire to move on," says Kathy Stokes, who co-owns the store in Steamboat Springs, Colorado, with her husband, Terry.

The collaboration among franchisees, and between franchisees and the corporate team in Denver has helped PostNet win a string of accolades. *Franchise Business Review* has repeatedly named PostNet a top franchise opportunity based on franchisee satisfaction scores, and *Entrepreneur* magazine has consistently ranked PostNet as a top opportunity.

Franchisees are able to offer a full range of printing services.

A Dynamic Business

Today's PostNet is the result of three decades of innovation and evolution driven by its founders.

Steve Greenbaum and Brian Spindel were pioneers in the pack-and-ship industry in the 1980s. Together they helped more than 400 people start their own independent mail and parcel businesses from 1985 to 1992.

By the early 1990s, the Gulf War and lagging U.S. economy were making it harder for independent businesses to compete, so Steve and Brian turned to franchising to create a global brand with robust systems and bargaining power that would deliver more value to owners. The PostNet franchise was founded in December 1992, with Steve as CEO and Brian as President and COO, the roles they still fill today.

From the beginning, the company innovated to stay ahead of the market. PostNet has one overall guiding principle, Steve says: "Our business will always evolve with consumer needs and technology."

PostNet added graphic design services and full-service printing at the turn of the millennium. It added marketing support services to help small businesses grow in 2003, unveiled a suite of online marketing solutions in 2012 and became one of the first franchise systems to offer 3D printing in 2014.

"Steve and Brian are great individuals who think outside the box," says Greg Claiborne, who has owned the PostNet in Round Rock, Texas, since 2003. "Steve and Brian are always anticipating opportunities and keeping us ahead of the curve."

The co-founders have made frequent appearances on Fox Business and other networks, and PostNet has been featured twice on the CBS hit show *Undercover Boss*.

Another thing that makes PostNet special: The company is radically transparent with potential franchisees. While many people agree that PostNet is an amazing franchise opportunity, you can evaluate the business yourself.

If you are looking for a franchise that values people, purpose, profit and forward-thinking business processes, PostNet may be right for you.

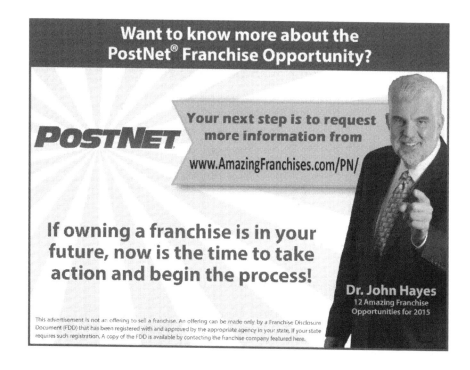

Just look at the awards and recognitions garnered by Wingstop:

* ❖ *Entrepreneur* magazine recognized the company in both its Franchise 500 and Fastest-Growing Chains edition;

* ❖ *Nation's Restaurant News* named the company a Top 100 Chain, and the #3 Top Growth Chain;

* ❖ *Fast Casual* ranked Wingstop among its Top 100 Movers and Shakers; and

* ❖ *QSR* listed the company among Best Franchise Deals, and the QSR 50.

Considering that those are just recent awards and recognitions, it's an amazing accomplishment!

Beyond all that, Wingstop is the fastest-growing chicken wing chain in America with 600 stores and counting. There's also the matter of 10 consecutive years of same-store sales growth, and now the international community is showing up to expand Wingstop overseas—the company has already pushed its boundaries into Russia.

Multi-unit operators are welcome as Wingstop will surpass 1,000 locations within the next three years. And if all that's not amazing enough, I suggest you go sample some of their wings!

—Dr. John P. Hayes

Wingstop: Flappin' about an Amazing Chicken Wing Franchise

When it comes to chicken wings, what's all the flap about? Americans consume 25 billion wings a year. It can't be rocket science. By sheer demand, anybody should be able to succeed in this so-called game of chicken, right?

Well, just ask McDonald's. They know a thing or two about franchising and food. So when the granddaddy of fast food decided to diversify the menu with chicken wings in 2013, it should have been a homerun. But think again.

Wingstop, one of the fastest-growing chicken wing chains in America, wasn't McScared. In fact, in the same year that McDonald's was talking wings, "The Wing Experts" at Wingstop, based in Dallas, Texas, posted historic growth of its franchise chain, opened its benchmark 600th location, chalked up its 10th consecutive year of same-store sales growth, and extended its international reach as far away as Russia.

Now that's amazing!

And Wingstop did all that without a drive-thru, heat lamps, or the proverbial, discounted dollar menu. In fact, legions of true wing fanatics continue to champion the

Wingstop business by driving to a restaurant, parking the car, going inside, and ordering and waiting—yes, waiting—for the food. That's right. Fresh wings, never frozen, cooked-to-order, has made Wingstop one heck of an amazing business. And to the die-hard wing connoisseur, it's made Wingstop a bonafide expert in the industry, too.

More than 600 locations and headed to 1,000 in the next three years!

Setting Historic Records

Oh, and that McDonald's idea kind of flew south just in time for winter. While Wingstop was setting historic records and inching ever closer to the $1 million goal for average unit volume (AUV), *The Wall Street Journal* was reporting that McDonald's was stuck with about 10 million pounds of unsold frozen wings by the end of 2013.

So, again, what's all the flap about?

Wingstop President and CEO Charlie Morrison has a wonderful answer. And it's a position that a burger giant like McDonald's will never own.

"I'm a big fan of the idea that sometimes a lack of innovation is a good thing," Morrison told *Nation's Restaurant News* (*NRN*) in 2013. "You don't have to be all things to all people. In fact, you can specialize and be more successful. Just execute flawlessly and stick to the aspects of your business that have made you the success that you are. I point to this theory when it comes to Wingstop and 10 years of same-store sales growth. We never lose sight of what got us to where we are. That's a true strategy. Our biggest introduction to the menu this year has been the launch of our Mango Habanero flavor. And the response has been off the charts. Our guests love it. It's new. It's delicious. And guess what? It sticks to exactly what we know. We only do wings."

Flynn Dekker, Chief Marketing Officer for Wingstop, shared the same sentiment with *NRN*, attributing the chain's success to being "hyper focused" on its target—18- to 24-year-olds—and sticking to what it knows: selling chicken.

Wingstop President and CEO Charlie Morrison: "We only do wings."

Amazing Brand Recognition

Perfecting one thing, delicious wings, has been consistent for Wingstop for 20 years. And as the brand celebrates a landmark anniversary of two decades of success, the future is more of the same, albeit on a bigger and more global scale.

Menu innovation has become a science with a goal to "bring flavor," as Wingstop continues to deliver one-of-a-kind flavor introductions to its award-winning wings. And the awards don't stop with the menu.

The growth of the Wingstop chain has earned the brand recognition, most recently in 2014, for *Entrepreneur* magazine's Franchise 500 and Fastest-Growing Chains, Technomic's Fastest-Growing Fast-Casual Chains, *NRN*'s Top 100 Chains and #3 Top Growth Chain, *Fast Casual*'s Top 100 Movers and Shakers, *QSR*'s Best Franchise Deals, and the *QSR* 50, just to name a few.

Chicagoland Wing Kings, LLC: Three of 10 partners pictured left to right—Asheesh Seth, Vishal Shah and Salil Contractor.

Multi-Unit Operators Welcome

Speaking of franchise deals, who is signing up to join this fast-casual wing sensation?

While the AUV keeps climbing on the Wingstop Franchise Disclosure Document, so do the leads from people interested in owning a Wingstop franchise...or 10...or 20...or even 50 locations.

In the beginning of any franchisor's story, there are the single-unit owner operators who bet the farm on an idea. And those early gamblers are still around at Wingstop, saucing and tossing the now-famous wings at their restaurants.

On Track for 1,000 Locations

Meanwhile, the return on investment is much more tangible these days. With an AUV of $974,000 and system-wide sales exceeding $550 million in 2013, the Wingstop opportunity is hotter than the Atomic sauce on the menu. With more than 675 open restaurants and commitments for more than 700 new locations, the Wingstop network is on track to surpass 1,000 locations in the next three years.

Thanks to an impressive 20-year track record in franchising, Wingstop has graduated from a household name in many markets to introducing its concept to many international markets. It also has elevated its profile with experienced operators. Today, many of the people who join the network are multi-brand, multi-unit franchisees. And the reputation that Wingstop has established now puts the franchise opportunity on the radar for talented restaurant investors looking to add to a portfolio of franchise brands under their management.

"The quality of our Brand Partners is exceptional," says Dekker, noting that top-notch franchisees also have attracted others to the brand.

Brand Partners Thrive

While the single-unit restaurant operators are still an incredible story of putting all the eggs in one basket (so to speak) with a Wingstop business, there are more stories these days of Brand Partners—the name that Wingstop crowns on its franchise owners—like the Chicagoland Wing Kings, LLC.

This franchisee of 10 partners growing the Wingstop brand in the greater Chicago area has earned its kingly status in franchise experience. The partners also own and operate more than 130 Dunkin Donuts locations. Following a franchise system is something that Chicagoland Wing Kings knows quite well. And focusing on a brand that has perfected its niche, like Dunkin has perfected the donut business, was just what attracted this group to Wingstop. The Brand Partner was well capitalized to open big with Wingstop, and Chicagoland Wing Kings has opened seven Wingstop restaurants in less than 24 months with a commitment for another five locations on the horizon. And they haven't stopped there.

"We are continuing to expand our Wingstop restaurants," says Vishal Shah, a partner with Chicagoland Wing Kings. "While I don't want to put a number on our expansion, my partners and I believe that 25 to 30 restaurants is possible."

And don't think this chicken idea can't fly just as fast overseas.

Taking Flight Worldwide

"One of the most exciting things we've done in the last two years is address a deliberate and very methodical approach to international growth," Morrison said. "This is a great time to start looking at the bigger picture."

Yes, Wingstop is officially a global opportunity. Recent expansion into Mexico, Russia, Singapore, the Philippines, Indonesia and United Arab Emirates is taking the Wingstop menu to all parts of the world. And the franchise opportunity has become a delicious investment in several languages.

Awarding large franchise agreements for as many as 50 locations in the Philippines and 100 locations in Indonesia, for example, where rapid development is in the works, will make a lasting international impression with customers.

"Following a record-breaking year of development in 2013, the demand for Wingstop continues to flourish around the globe," explains Wingstop's Chief Development Officer Dave Vernon.

Sticking to the Basics

Recent headlines have Wingstop opening more than 100 new restaurants in 2014, another company record.

"We want to build on that momentum," Vernon told the *Dallas Business Journal*. "We're going to focus on the basics—good real estate, good franchise partners and serving good food."

And that's a lot to flap about.

Amazing Franchise Tools

Match Your Personality to the Appropriate Franchise Opportunities

Use Franchising to Get Your U.S. Green Card

Franchise Definitions

Franchise Resources

Match Your Personality to the Appropriate Franchise Opportunities

One of the most important lessons that I learned as a franchisor is that franchisees are not all created equally. Actually, I learned that lesson early on in my franchising career, but as a franchisor I realized what it really meant, and more importantly, I realized that many franchisee failures, and many of the situations that result in disgruntled franchisor/franchisee relationships, could be avoided if people paid attention to this lesson.

Failed Franchisees Missed this Lesson

In fact, this is one of the most important lessons that you, as a prospective franchisee, can learn about franchising, and the sooner you do something about it, the more likely you are to succeed as a franchisee. Do yourself the favor that many franchisees before you did not do—learn this lesson and follow it!

Every franchisor should pay attention to this lesson, too, and implement the steps that will help their franchisees succeed. But there's another pertinent lesson you should know about: Franchisors are not all created equally!

My Personal Experience with Profiling

In my case, here's what happened. The founder of the company where I eventually served as President and CEO died unexpectedly. Ken D'Angelo was a magnificent person, and one of the most conscientious franchisors, and unfortunately he died at a time when his company was moving from a start-up to a professionally run organization. He had developed a time-tested operating system, the only one of its kind that taught people from all walks of life how to buy and sell real estate for a profit.

To Ken, investing in real estate was akin to crossing a busy highway—you had to study the situation, calculate the variables, know where to look and what to look for, and ultimately know when to step out and seize the moment. And to Ken, who had no formal education beyond high school, anyone could follow his amazing system and succeed as a real estate investor. And many people did (especially while subprime lending existed).

When I succeeded Ken, at his request in 2004, we had some 250 franchisees buying almost 10,000 houses a year in 30-some states. Every year, Ken organized an annual meeting where he and others provided additional insights about real estate investing, as well as training, networking, and awards. Lots of awards. Real estate investors come with big egos—most franchisees come with big egos!—and a good way to keep them happy and engaged in your business is to publicly reward them for their achievements. Ken was giving his top performing franchisees Ford F-150 pickup trucks, as well as trophies and cash. But now here's the odd twist: The top franchisees weren't necessarily getting the best awards.

Identifying Top Franchisees

Who's a top franchisee? That's no different than asking any business owner: Who's your best customer? Sadly, most business owners, including franchisors, can't answer that question accurately, so it's not surprising that Ken couldn't, either. In any business, the best customer is the one who comes back time after time and pays you (the business owner) the most money without disrupting your business.

For example, I once had a client who paid my agency more money per month than any other client—at least when he paid. However, he was so obnoxious to my people that any time he called no one would talk to him, which meant that I had to handle every detail for him. Well, he wasn't paying *that* much money, and I fired him. I couldn't afford his disruptions to my business.

When Ken decided to reward franchisees, he looked at several qualifiers, but essentially he rewarded those who bought the most houses in a year's time. Made sense to me, but for some reason one day I asked our financial folks to provide me with a list of franchisees ranked by royalty value.

In other words, I said, show me the franchisees in ranked order with the one who paid us the most money in royalties at #1 on the list, and the one who paid us the least money in royalties at #250 (or whatever number was last place) on the list.

"Do We Know these Franchisees?"

When I got the list I said to my leadership team: *Who are these people at the top of the list?*

They were not the franchisees we had been awarding year after year. Some were, but most were not. In fact, I had never met some of the franchisees, and in the four years that I had worked closely with Ken, he never mentioned them to me, and I don't think he ever visited them in their markets (and we visited many franchisees every year).

Turns out the top franchisees may also be those you rarely hear from...they do not complain, they do not make requests, they do not (necessarily) want to speak at your meetings and conventions, they do not demand that you come and visit them...they just work the system and, well, make money!

The Top Franchisee Report, as I started referring to that list, triggered a goldmine of information and provided tremendous insight for how we should spend our time as a franchisor. For example, our operations folks spent an inordinate amount of time helping many of the lower-rung franchisees that never seemed to be able to work our system.

We thought that if we spent more time (and money) coaching, training, and encouraging these franchisees, they might eventually catch on and perform better...but there was little evidence of that.

The fact was, the best way to help some of those bottom-rung franchisees was to find a buyer for their franchise and let them move on to another occupation. They were simply not fit for our business, and we should not have sold them a franchise.

"What's Different about these Franchisees?"

After I got over my initial surprise about the contents of the list I asked another question: *Why these franchisees?*

Now I wanted to know why the top 25 franchisees were the top 25 franchisees. Why them, and not the bottom 25? Obviously the top 25 paid us the most money. But what were they doing that the bottom 25 were not doing? Or, why were the top 25 so much more capable than the bottom 25?

Best of all I asked: What can we do to make sure we only award our franchises to people who will show up in the top 25?

There were numerous answers to that question, but one of the most pertinent was: *Assess their personalities to make sure they're a fit for our business.* Actually, Ken had already been doing that, but now it was time to pay more attention to the results.

How to Use Your Assessment

Enough about my experience. What's most important here is that you pay attention to the results that you can generate from a personality assessment.

You do not need a franchisor to provide the results to you...you can get the results yourself. Franchisors use different personality survey tools, and I have arranged for you to get a free personality assessment from the top two organizations that work with franchisors. Keep reading!

ConnectMe

Powered by Franchise Navigator, ConnectMe is a market-validated profiling tool that has helped thousands of people to better understand their skills, values and needs as they relate to franchise ownership, according to Craig Slavin, who oversees the holding company that promotes Connect-Me.

The survey takes no more than 10 minutes to complete as it asks a variety of questions, including where you would like to own and operate a franchise, and how much money you anticipate investing in a franchise. I especially like that ConnectMe matches your responses to the responses received from the top performing franchisees of many different franchise companies. In that way, ConnectMe matches "people to people" and not "people to businesses."

The assessment helps you better understand the types of businesses that not only value what you value, but require your specific skills and provide a system that meets your needs.

It's easy to complete the survey, just go to my affiliate link, www.navigatorsurvey.com/survey/HAYES.html, and follow the instructions.

Franchise Success Strategies

Through years of development and implementation, Dynamic Performance Systems discovered that there are seven characteristics that are critical to a franchisee's success. Prior to this knowledge, and the assessment that has been built around it, there was no accurate and scientific way to help a franchise candidate learn how to find an appropriate franchise opportunity, reports Fred Berni, president of Dynamic Performance Systems, which administers Franchise Success Strategies.

Today, with 25 years of experience, hundreds of franchise companies have relied on the FranchiZe Profile to identify which candidates have the best chance of succeeding in their business. Franchise Success Strategies has distilled knowledge gained from its franchise client base and makes this information available to franchise candidates.

The Franchise Success Strategies report tells you about the seven characteristics critical to franchising success, why the strategies are important, and what training and self-development would be helpful to you to improve your chances of succeeding as a franchisee. Essentially, the report will help you decide what kind of business will be best for you based on your job-specific needs and behaviors.

Completing the survey is easy; just click on my affiliate link, tinyurl.com/qcz6btk, answer nine simple questions, and one free Success Strategy will appear on your computer screen, and it also will be emailed to you.

DISC Offers a Free Assessment

While the DISC Personality Profile is not franchise specific, it provides interesting insights about an individual's strengths characterized in terms of Dominance, Influence, Steadiness and Compliance.

A Dominant personality, for example, might do well in a business that depends on the franchisee to generate sales; a Compliant personality probably would not succeed in such a business. However, a Compliant personality might do well in a service business that interacts closely with customers, while a Dominant personality might not succeed in such a business.

It takes about 10 minutes to complete the DISC assessment and numerous companies provide it for free. Search for "free disc profile" and you'll find one. Some franchisors use DISC to help them select franchisees, but many more use Franchise Success Strategies and ConnectMe.

There's no reason why you should not use all three assessments, especially since they are free.

Give Yourself an Edge

Franchise companies do not need to rely on personality profiling to be amazing, but amazing franchisors are always interested in a franchise candidate's profiling results. So share your results. Of course, many franchisors will ask you to complete their preferred, sometimes proprietary assessment, and you should be happy to do so.

Using personality assessments and matching the results to appropriate franchise opportunities levels the playing field and ultimately helps you succeed in franchising.

Foreign Investors:

Use Franchising to Get Your U.S. Green Card

Franchising has recently become a fast track opportunity for foreign investors who want to move to the United States. Thousands of foreign investors have already taken advantage of the Immigrant Investor Program administered by the U.S. Citizenship and Immigration Services (USCIS), and the number of applicants is rising dramatically in part due to favorable changes in the program, and in part due to franchising.

Known as EB-5, the program was created to stimulate the U.S. economy through job creation and capital investment by foreign investors. Essentially, a qualified foreigner invests $500,000 directly into a business, such as any of the 12 amazing franchise opportunities in this eBook, or into a regional fund that invests in businesses, and gets a green card and eventually U.S. citizenship providing that the investment created at least 10 full-time jobs for at least two years.

You Can Move Your Family to the U.S.

Foreign investors are using EB-5 to move their families to the U.S., or to send their children to the U.S. to study. A married investor, for example, gets visas for himself, his spouse, and all unmarried children under the age of 21. While the program has been slow to get off the ground—it has existed since 1990—more than $4 billion was invested in 2013 alone, and interest has spiked in part due to franchising.

Look around the U.S. and you'll find foreigners operating many franchised businesses. Of course, America exists because of industrious foreigners, and franchisors welcome them because they are enthusiastic about learning a successful operating system that they and their family members can use to change their lives for the better. However, EB-5 does not require investors to actually work in a business; after investing their money, foreign investors can live wherever they choose, start their own business, take a job, or retire!

A Means for U.S. Expansion

Any U.S. franchisor today that isn't aware of EB-5 is missing a huge opportunity for expansion. Many American franchisors are focused on international expansion—they want to sell master licenses to foreigners who will build out the franchise brand in their own countries—but EB-5 provides an opportunity to build more franchises in the U.S.

with foreign capital and expertise. While many franchise companies are unaware of this opportunity, that will soon change because franchising is a small community and news travels fast.

What's the Red Tape?

Of course, as with any bureaucratic program, there are numerous requirements and regulations with EB-5, and it's not simply a matter of popping half-a-million dollars into a franchisor's bank account on Friday afternoon and moving the family to the U.S. during the weekend. The investor must prove his or her money came from a lawful source, and must also pass the scrutiny of U.S. immigration investors. The U.S. is for sale, but not to criminals and terrorists.

In addition, the investment must create tangible employment: at least 10 permanent full-time jobs for two years. However, indirect or induced jobs count, and that's where franchising holds the trump card.

A Match for Franchising

Originally, most of the EB-5 money was invested into real estate projects that may or may not have created the requisite employment. But $500,000 invested into certain franchised businesses can create upwards of 40 jobs, including induced jobs that result from the supply chain.

Consider what happens, for example, when a new convenience store, such as Farm Stores, opens in a neighborhood. There are direct jobs—created for people to work in the store—and indirect jobs—created in the supply chain. Every Farm Stores unit needs milk, donuts, eggs, coffee, cups, straws, baked goods, bags, etc. Those requirements create new jobs. Plus there are induced jobs created by the payroll spend in the local market, and USCIS takes all of those jobs into account to qualify an investor.

Multi-Unit Operators to Benefit

If an investor doesn't want to be a franchisee, he doesn't have to be. Again, franchising is perfect for this program. In many franchise networks, there are multi-unit operators, or would-be multi-unit operators, who seek expansion capital, and sometimes partners. And once again, most of these operators have never heard of EB-5, but they will (through books such as this, through media, and through their franchise networks), and they'll want to know how to find these investors.

Meanwhile, LCR Capital, based in Connecticut, is a new EB-5 regional center that is making it easy to pair investors and franchise opportunities. An investor has to be concerned about creating those 10 permanent, full-time jobs. If his investment fails, or falls short of the requirement within two to three years, he and his family will be returning to their country of origin, sans $500,000! LCR Capital provides some assurance (but not a guarantee) that the investment will produce as required.

Invest Through a Regional EB-5 Center

"An investor can direct his money into a specific franchise business, which he can also operate," explains Suresh Rajan, founder and CEO of LCR Capital, "but he may be better off placing his money with a regional center that allows for the smart deployment of capital with strong franchise brands and existing operators. This option provides some assurance that the job creation will occur successfully," and the investor's visa won't be revoked.

LCR Capital, through EB-5 investors, is providing "five-year money" to existing multi-unit operators to develop new units of recognized franchise brands. "Instead of an investor having his green card and his capital contingent on the performance of one franchised store," continues Rajan, "his investment is spread over 200 to 300 stores, so there's a small likelihood of failure."

Timing is everything, and in the case of EB-5 and franchising, now is the time. However, this program takes time—from the moment an investor learns of the program, finds an investment vehicle, i.e. a franchise opportunity, or a regional center, and completes the USCIS documentation, six months to a year may pass. But to many investors, that's a very short time, and a small price to pay, to gain access to life in the United States. Still, investors should hurry because the program is up for review in 2015 and it's anticipated that the investment will be increased to $850,000 or even $1 million.

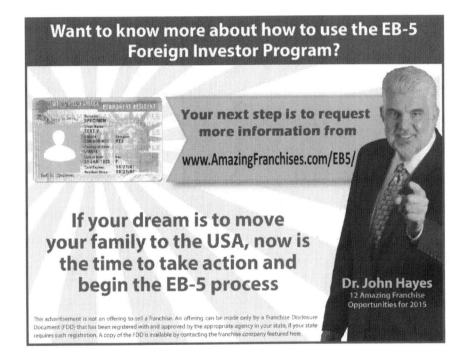

Franchise Definitions

Here are some of the most common terms used in franchising.

Advertising Fee: Many franchise opportunities require franchisees to pay a monthly fee into an Advertising or Marketing Fund. The fee is generally represented as a percentage (for example, two percent) and is almost always calculated on the franchisee's gross sales, as opposed to net sales or profits. The Advertising Fee may also be a flat fee. The Advertising Fee is ongoing and will be collected throughout the period of time the franchise agreement is in effect. Advertising Fund monies are used to advertise the franchise brand, its products and/or services.

Ad Fund: Franchisees pay their Advertising Fees into an Ad Fund, which is used to underwrite the cost of advertising and promotions for franchisees.

Disclosure: In some countries, and especially in the United States, franchisors are *required* by federal and some state laws to "disclose" individuals who are serious about acquiring a franchise. Disclosure is a process that includes providing prospective franchisees with a copy of the franchisor's Franchise Disclosure Document (FDD) and Franchise Agreement. The FDD must be delivered to a franchise candidate at least 14 days prior to the candidate purchasing the franchise. Disclosure minimizes fraudulent sales in franchising and promotes the safety and longevity of franchising.

Disclosure Document: See Franchise Disclosure Document.

Earnings Claim: An Earnings Claim may be included in a franchisor's Franchise Disclosure Document. An Earnings Claim documents the earnings of franchisees in the franchisor's network. *Most franchisors do not include Earnings Claims in their documents.* Those who do not are prohibited from making any oral or written statements concerning the actual or potential sales, costs, income or profits of their franchise opportunities.

Franchise: It's a license that grants an individual or an entity, i.e. a corporation, the right to use a franchisor's system for the purpose of marketing, selling and distributing the franchisor's products and/or services.

Franchise Agreement: A legal document (license) signed by both the franchisor and the Franchisee granting the franchisee the right to operate the franchise system for a specified period of time, in a specified format and sometimes in a specified location.

Franchise Associations: There are approximately 40 trade associations throughout the world that represent the interests of franchisors and franchisees. See International Franchise Association.

Franchise Disclosure Document (FDD): Every franchisor in the United States is required to complete and maintain a Franchise Disclosure Document (FDD). The FDD, in layperson's language, describes the franchise opportunity. The Items of disclosure are standard for all franchise companies. There are 23 Items that require disclosure, including: Litigation, Initial Franchise Fee, Franchisee's Obligations, Franchisor's Obligations, Territory, Restrictions on What the Franchisee May Sell, Renewal, Termination, Transfer and Dispute Resolution, List of Outlets (Franchisees), Financial Statements, and more!

Franchisee: The individual or entity, i.e. a corporation, that's assigned the rights to a franchise.

Franchise Expo: Franchise companies come together under one roof to exhibit their franchise opportunities for a day or more. The public is invited to these events. Expos sometimes include educational programs.

Franchise Fee: A one-time, upfront fee required by the franchisor.

Franchise Portal: A website that promotes franchise opportunities and may also include educational information about franchising.

Franchisor: The company that grants franchises to franchisees.

International Franchise Association: IFA is the world's largest trade organization representing both franchisors and franchisees. Their headquarters is in Washington, D.C. and their website is www.Franchise.org.

International Franchise Expo: The world's premier event among franchise expos is sponsored by the International Franchise Association. The producer of the IFE is MFV Expositions. Their website is www.IFEInfo.com.

Royalty Fee: A payment of money by the franchisee to the franchisor. Usually represented as a percentage (as an example, six percent) and paid weekly or monthly. May also be a flat weekly or monthly fee. Royalties are almost always paid on the franchisee's gross sales, as opposed to net sales or profits. This is an ongoing fee that must be paid during the period of time the franchise agreement/license is in effect.

Franchise Resources

The following list provides information about resources that may be of assistance to you. Inclusion does not carry with it any endorsement by the author. The list is not exhaustive, but it includes major resources. Search the web for additional information, some of which may be more current than items on the list.

Franchise Associations

International Franchise Association
1501 K Street N.W., Suite 350
Washington, DC 20005
Telephone: 202-628-8000
Website: www.Franchise.org

In addition to representing franchisors and franchisees, the IFA also represents the Council of Franchise Suppliers, which includes attorneys, accountants, consultants, franchise brokers, and others who may be able to assist you in your exploration of franchising. IFA promotes numerous books and other resources about franchising, and publishes *Franchising World* magazine. Free resources are included on the IFA's website.

Canadian Franchise Association
116-5399 Eglinton Avenue West
Toronto, Ontario
Canada M9C 5K6
Telephone: 416-695-2896
E-mail: info@cfa.ca
Website: www.CFA.ca

For a list of Franchise Associations Worldwide:

www.Franchise.org

Franchise Expositions

MFV Expositions
Telephone: 201-226-1130
Website: www.MFVExpo.com

In addition to the International Franchise Expo, MFV Expositions produces the West Coast Franchise Expo, Franchise Expo South and international franchise events including *Feria Internactional De Franquicias* in Mexico City.

Franchise Portals

FranchiseExpo.com, www.FranchiseExpo.com
Bison, www.Bison.com
Entrepreneur, www.Entrepreneur.com
Franchise, www.Franchise.com

Franchise Opportunities, www.FranchiseOpportunities.com
Franchise Solutions, www.FranchiseSolutions.com
The Franchise Handbook, www.Franchise1.com

U.S. Government Resources

U.S. Small Business Administration:
www.SBAonline.sba.gov/
U.S. Commerce Department International Trade Administration: www.ITA.doc.gov

Publications

Bond's Franchise Guide
Entrepreneur, publishes the Franchise 500 every January
Franchise Handbook, www.FranchiseHandbook.com
Franchise Opportunities Guide, www.Franchise.org
Franchise Times, www.FranchiseTimes.com
Franchise Update, www.Franchise-Update.com
Franchising World, www.Franchise.org

Author's Biography

Dr. John P. Hayes

Your Personal Franchise Coach

John Hayes is one of the few people in the world to have been a franchisee, a franchisor, and an advisor to franchisors and franchisees. For many years John's client list included the International Franchise Association (IFA), the International Franchise Expo (IFE), and dozens of franchise companies.

For nearly 30 years he has taught the most popular symposium at the International Franchise Expo: "The A to Zs of Buying a Franchise." John teaches marketing and management courses at Gulf University for Science & Technology in Kuwait, and he blogs about franchising at www.HowToBuyAFranchise.com.

He coaches prospective franchisees and franchisors, and you can schedule a private Skype session with him by visiting the coaching page of his blog at www.HowToBuy-AFranchise.com/franchise-coaching/.

Two More eBooks
You Might Enjoy...

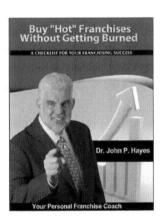 

Buy "Hot" Franchises Without Getting Burned

www.amazon.com/dp/B00EPFSXV4/

101 Questions To Ask
Before You Invest In A Franchise

www.amazon.com/dp/B00EYT5BB6/

BizComPress

Want to Publish Your Book?

Do you have a story to tell that will help others improve their life, their business, or otherwise make a difference? BizCom Press can help you reach the widest audience possible. Founded by authors for authors, BizCom Press is a new kind of publishing company. Our award-winning team will help you write your book, edit it, design it, publish it, and promote it. And you keep the majority of your earnings!

Whether you already have a manuscript, or just the seed of an idea, contact us and we'll provide honest feedback based on decades of experience in book publishing. If we believe the manuscript or the idea has a market, we can develop a plan that fits your budget and you'll be on your way to becoming a published author.

For more information contact Scott White at 214-458-5751 or Scott@BizComPress.com.

Made in the USA
Lexington, KY
06 April 2015